CLOSER TO HOME

the author and the author portrait

TERENCE BYRNES

Véhicule Press

ACKNOWLEDGEMENTS

I owe a great deal to the visual and editorial insights of Patricia Woodburn, to my warm professional associations with Margaret Goldik and Ian McGillis at the Montreal Review of Books, *to the cheerful assistance of Lori Schubert at the Quebec Writers' Federation, and to Ian Ferrier, for having offered the project a second life.*

Published with the generous assistance of The Canada Council for the Arts, the Book Publishing Industry Development Program of the Department of Canadian Heritage and the Société de développement des entreprises culturelles du Québec (SODEC).

Véhicule Press appreciates the assistance and collaboration of Concordia University's Faculty of Arts and Science.

BOOK DESIGN Marc Elias
PRINTING Marquis Book Printing Inc.

Dépôt légal, Bibliothèque nationale du Québec and
the National Library of Canada, fourth trimester 2008

Library and Archives Canada Cataloguing in Publication
Byrnes, Terence, 1948 –
Closer to home : the author and the author portrait / Terence Byrnes.
ISBN 978-1-55065-248-2 (PAPER) ISBN 978-1-55065-250-5 (CLOTH)
1. Byrnes, Terence, 1948- . 2. Authors, Canadian (English)—Québec (Province)—Montréal—Portraits. 3. Authors, Canadian (English)—Québec (Province)—Montréal—Anecdotes. 4. Portrait photography--Québec (Province)—Montréal. I. Title.
TR681.A85B97 2008 C810.9'0054 C2008-904256-5

Published by Véhicule Press, Montréal, Québec, Canada
WWW.VEHICULEPRESS.COM

Distribution in Canada by LitDistCo
orders@litdistco.ca

Distribution in U.S. by Independent Publishers Group
WWW.IPGBOOK.COM

PRINTED IN CANADA

for Patricia and Erin

"I can say that… I found pictures trying to show people in their natural circumstances generally disappointing."

IRVING PENN
Worlds in a Small Room

contents

CLOSER TO HOME

the author and the author portrait

THE IMAGINED PORTRAIT

> Could you believe me without? I had no portrait, now, but am small, like the wren; and my hair is bold like the chestnut bur; and my eyes, like the sherry in the glass, that the guest leaves. Would this do just as well?
>
> EMILY DICKINSON, 1862
> *in response to a request for a photographic portrait*

I BEGAN MAKING PORTRAITS IN A SMALL, profoundly depressed American city that had abandoned its commercially deserted downtown to the poor. One day, I was rummaging in the last store—a junk shop—on one of its dying streets and discovered a hatbox jumbled with lapel pins and buttons, political campaign memorabilia, and advertising giveaways, including a Chinese-style fan that spread to reveal a loaf of Butternut bread. The earliest lapel button commemorated the Chicago World's Fair of 1883 while a hammer-and-sickle stickpin spoke of more recent times. What really caught my eye, though, was a tiny white button displaying the portrait of a curly-haired young man gazing into the distance. The legend that curved around the bottom edge read "P.B. Shelley English Poet." I had no idea why Shelley's picture would turn up almost 150 years after his death and come to rest in the United States between a Butternut bread fan and a Soviet icon, but I spent a dime and bought it.

The people I photographed in the city lived on welfare or whatever temporary, hardscrabble jobs they could find. Their innocence of the world, beyond what the usual network of family connections might bring, was unsettling. Although they would hail me on the street by calling out "Canada!" not all of them knew what, or where, Canada actually was. Some were equally innocent of the everyday aspects of having a photograph made. They would stand, spread their legs, let their mouths hang slightly open, and stare past the camera. A woman who lived in a house so tiny that I had to step outside her front door to photograph her inside the house told me that she and her husband had been married for 12 years, but had no family pictures. A 13-year-old Appalachian girl serving hamburgers with her mother in a diner looked incredulously at an 8" x 10" print of another girl, turned to her mother, and asked, "Mama, he goin' draw me like that?"

I also met people who understood portraiture better than I did; they knew they had to assume a role for it. Some young girls I photographed spontaneously bounced down to sit on their heels, open their legs, crook their elbows, and place their fingertips on the insides of their thighs in imitation of a local country singer. When the gangster style began to dominate entertainment-world representations of black America, friendly young black people unhesitatingly assumed expressions of stony contempt. Latinos sometimes refused to have their faces photographed but were happy to lift a shirt to show the tattooed face of the Virgin Mary or Jesus on their chests.

I began to realize just how strange and unnatural portraits are. They ask the person being photographed to draw on deep, or shallow, cultural resources to comply with the very idea of being portrayed. To sit for a portrait, we first have to discern what we're sitting for and how long it takes. Is it a painting? A pencil drawing? A photograph? Having identified the form, we must then decide the way we wish to be seen, which requires us to refer to other images. If we have few or none to refer to, we're reduced to the most basic components of self, our unposed, slack-jawed faces and awkward bodies. The portraitist can guide us and position us, as the *Vogue* fashion photographer Irving Penn artfully did in his field studies of Dahomey fetishists and New Guinea mud men, but what does the portrait then show, the subject or the pose?

While trying to answer that question for myself, I ran across reproductions of Roman wall paintings and ceramics from Herculaneum, the Roman city that was lost in the same volcanic eruption that destroyed Pompeii. These frequently beautiful images of theatrical scenes, mythological figures, and daily life were published in book form in the eighteenth century and sparked a neo-classical movement in Western art. Among the Herculaneum frescoes, I saw groups of figures assembled into a fluid visual whole by the sumptuous folds of their clothing and careful positioning of their arms so that one figure leads effortlessly (if not quite naturally) to the next. Another fresco depicts a seated female figure who symbolizes Arcadia, the mythological Greek land of peace, order, and harmony. She grasps a staff in her left hand while her right forefinger touches her temple. Her other fingers are loosely spread and fall elegantly from her cheek to her upper neck. It's an artist's arrangement of the body, not one copied from life.

Penn's field studies of native peoples suddenly made a new kind of sense to me, as did portraiture in general. Penn used principles of design that were unrelated to his subjects as people, but were of a piece with ancient traditions of design. Arcadia's hand, staff, and gown convey her meaning, not her personality. The single or group portrait, as the frescoes make clear, is distinct from other kinds of portrayal (think of caricature, forensic documentation, photographic grab shots, or life masks), ancient, or current. It has its own, distinct species of artificiality.

The literary portrait is a special case of portraiture whose origins also reach to the distant past. For most of the last few millennia, the audible voice of the poet or the actor was the principal vehicle of literature. As the periodic appearance of newly discovered "portraits" of Shakespeare or Emily Dickinson attest, we haven't lost the desire for some physical manifestation of the author to embody the abstraction of print. The British art historian Andrew Piper traces the history of the connection between text and author to at least the fifth century B.C., when statues of long-dead poets began to appear in public settings. By the third century the conventions of portraiture in bronze and stone—including facial expression, angle of the head, and the posture of the body—were firmly established. They became part of what Piper characterizes as "the astonishing continuity of the tradition of recording and preserving the images of poets."

By the seventeenth century, the author portrait had become an ordinary embellishment in books, usually in the form of an engraved frontispiece whose presence gave body to the silent voice of the text (which became increasingly silent as more people became literate and didn't need to gather publicly to hear work read, although reading out loud in private was still a common practice). A century later, celebrity and sexuality began to take their places in the creation of an author's identity, and the famous paintings made of Byron (dressed, for instance, in the putative costume of a native Albanian, sheathed short sword in the crook of his arm) don't stint on beauty, melancholy, or drama. Byron appears to have been quite aware of how to pose for different forms of portrayal. Sitting for a sculpture portrait, he claimed to dislike the look of the laureate wreath ("I won't have my head garnished like a Christmas pie with holly…"), but his sculptor said he nonetheless "[put on] a quite different expression from that usual to him." We can only assume that, had Byron never seen a portrait sculpture, he would have had no idea of the kind of expression he would want to assume.

When photography was invented in the 1830s, it was received as an unprecedented and sometimes vaguely threatening extension of technology into both art and science. Baudelaire, who was both prescient and conservative about the changes photography would bring, saw it as demeaning to the art of painting and as a "democratic" threat to both art and history. The American painter (and, later, telegrapher) Samuel Morse visited Louis Daguerre's photographic studio in Paris and discovered in the daguerreotype a natural science, "a new field of research into the depth of microscopic Nature." He, among others, imagined that the world could be investigated in a photograph by examining it with powerful magnifying lenses.

The photographic image captured and preserved something for a nineteenth century viewer that was, like DNA today, a disturbingly intimate and complete record of nature. Balzac, for instance, didn't like to be photographed because he believed that the process removed a thin layer of skin to produce an image. Elizabeth Barrett Browning wrote, in the first decade of photography's existence, that a portrait caught "the very shadow of the person lying there fixed forever!" Her language brings to mind a funeral viewing, but one which suspends endlessly that moment of the casket's closing and consequent interment.

When the photographic negative was invented (only 27 years after Byron's death and during the period of American romanticism), allowing multiple prints of an image, the appearance of celebrity came within almost everyone's reach. Ordinary people engaged in a mad rush to buy *cartes de visite*—pictures of themselves, of the famous, or even of recently deceased loved ones—so they could distribute them to their friends. Painters of small keepsake portraits, once a thriving industry, either went out of business or became photographers.

By the end of the century, in a world that was quickly becoming glutted with realistic images, the author portrait frontispiece had become an old-fashioned device. In Henry James's *The Portrait of a Lady*, for instance, Isabel Archer's innocence is signalled by her willingness to be "guided in the selection [of books] chiefly by the frontispiece."

Despite these millennia of tradition, which would seem at least to offer variety, contemporary author portraiture tends to make pretty dull art. Writers don't move much, or very interestingly, while they're going about the business of writing. And their public performances—if standing still and reading out loud in a bookstore count as such—are usually less than sexy, unless the writer has already established star appeal.

Five minutes spent examining the dust jackets in a bookstore show the contemporary author portrait as a curious little museum of poses and anti-poses. Formality is either ignored, as in the carefully unstudied snapshot, or the writer is lionized and pinned in place by devices such as the Arcadian touch at the forehead, or the chin resting on lightly curled fingers. The great majority of these writers might as well have been dead for centuries and fancifully revived to be displayed on a book jacket just as Homer is brought back to life in countless sculptures, paintings, and engravings.

During the course of photographing and writing this book, I found that men and women have different views about the value and meaning of their images. This accounts for the smaller number of women in *Closer to Home* despite the fact that there is no shortage of women writers. Young women will spontaneously rest their chins on their folded hands and gaze into the camera as readily as anyone, but they also enjoy being liberated from that role and told to do nothing in particular except chat with the photographer. In this case, their youthful attractiveness is all the authority and dignity they need. If they can be said to perform a role for the portrait or portraitist, it's the role of someone who is free.

Men in general are easier to portray because our culture's history has given us many images of men that would seem to be unflattering but leave their dignity intact and even enhance their sexual attractiveness. A man can be raggedly unshaven, slouch disinterestedly, or sneer, and enjoy being seen in the light of his Byronic rebelliousness, like Count Lara, whose "vital scorn of all" fixes the type. If a man doesn't look physically fit, dressing well makes the sins of the body disappear because his status is implied by his taste or his ability to buy expensive clothing. And if he dresses poorly and isn't conventionally handsome, a variety of other "looks," from the biker, to the slacker, to the cool nerd, are all sanctioned (thus, made admirable) by Hollywood films.

Women who do not have a sense of their lasting attractiveness as they age don't enjoy the same freedom. For some, the mere fact of being a photographic subject is a severe emotional trial. A woman writer who contracted pneumonia told me she was relieved to be bedridden because it gave her a valid excuse to call off our shoot. Others simply denied permission to use their images in the book, citing reasons that ranged from photographs that incidentally showed chipped paint on a baseboard to the admirably direct assessment, "It doesn't flatter me enough."

Appearance is obviously an important part of life, and only a fool would deny the relationship between a woman's status and her appearance. Still, it's disheartening to discover that clichés are the surest way to retain the appearance of the authority and dignity that literary success seems to demand. My favorite literary portrait demonstrating this is Irving Penn's 1951 photograph of Colette. She appears to be reclining and is wrapped up in what looks like a velvet blanket. Penn's angle was low, as though the camera were sitting on Colette's stomach. Her sleeves are large and floppy and, cocooned as she is in the blanket, she looks dressed for the sick room. Penn has separated her voluminous and curly hair so that her rather high forehead is exposed, something Colette hated.

Yet, she put up with it, presumably because of the photographer's name and his well-known work with *Vogue* magazine. It's Colette's right hand that gives the game away, though. Whether by Penn's direction or her own choice, it is folded awkwardly into a fist on which she rests her chin, as though this recourse to the image of Arcadian tranquility will rescue the dignity she feels to be at risk.

The brief written portraits that accompany these images are a response to the fragility of meaning that is produced by the clinical accuracy of photography. Emily Dickinson was well aware of this fragility when, in the same letter explaining that she had no portrait of herself, she wrote:

> It often alarms father. He says death might occur and he has moulds of all the rest, but has no mould of me; but I noticed the quick wore off those things, in a few days, and forestall the dishonor. You will think no caprice of me.

Of course, Dickinson's explanation held considerable caprice as well as insight. The "quick" of character does leave photographs almost immediately while writing retains it stubbornly.

In general, the photographs I have taken for this book don't pretend to be about character except in the sense that they reveal a face the subject allows to be shown. Celebrity was not a principle of choice, nor was literary merit (although there was a great deal of that). Instead, I wanted to portray writers away from the studio and to satisfy the ancient wish to see those who write for us.

TERENCE BYRNES
Montreal, 2008

CLOSER TO HOME

the author and the author portrait

IAN FERRIER IN HIS LIVING ROOM ON RUE LAVAL, PLATEAU MONT-ROYAL, DECEMBER 2007

WHEN IAN'S WIFE LET ME IN, he was out of sight in his basement explaining recording techniques to a visitor who stood at the top of the stairs. As I waited, I looked for locations to shoot. The house, with its towering ceilings, wide staircase to the second floor, and its displays of domesticity and art—from a long table piled with clothing to an eight-foot-high wooden feather mounted on the wall—looked as much like an artist's studio as it did a home. The basement housed castoffs, books (at one end, subjects from cichlids to astronomy, while at the other, Jack London to Oriana Fallaci), and a recording studio on a desk littered with CDs and vintage electronic paraphernalia. I made a number of photographs in which Ian was lost in extraneous detail before we moved upstairs. Ian's disconcertingly intense expression misrepresents him (although it's not necessarily a bad image for a writer to have). He is, if anything, gentlemanly and soft-spoken. When he saw this photograph, he said, "Looks like I'd eat your breakfast, and then tell you I was still hungry."

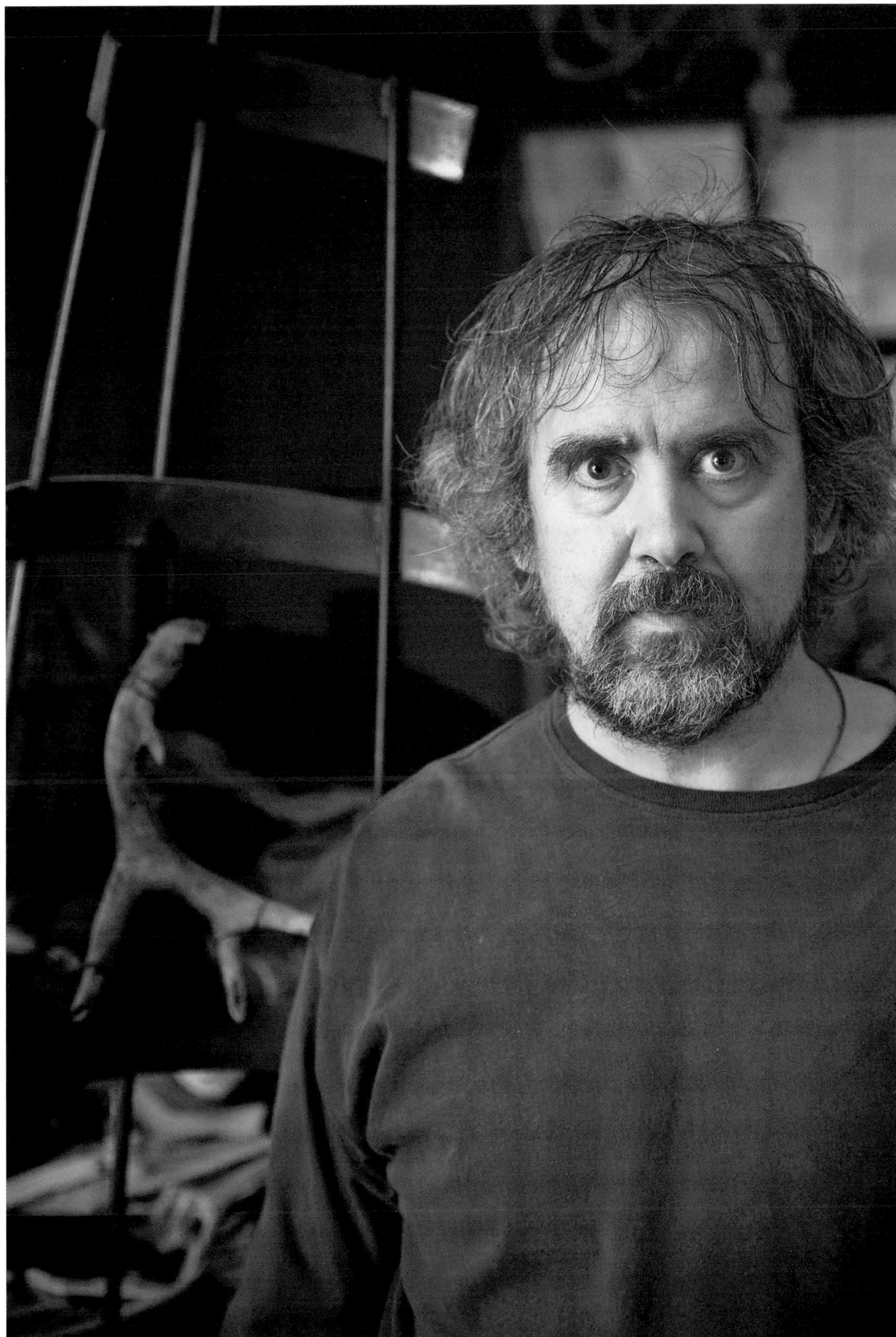

HEATHER O'NEILL IN HER RUE ST-URBAIN APARTMENT, PLATEAU MONT-ROYAL, DECEMBER 2007

HEATHER O'NEILL LIVED with her twelve-year-old daughter in a typical Plateau apartment with small rooms branching off a long hallway that leads to a kitchen. The front room, Heather's office, held a cheval glass, an iBook with cycling baby pictures on the screen, and a drawing of the planet Saturn on a blackboard. The living room displayed quirky art, porcelain curios, and a television whose picture was paused at a screen promising the first three episodes of the fourth season of *The Wire*. Heather's daughter's room contained an extraordinary collection of dolls crammed side by side on a display rack. Golden ringlets, Heidi pigtails, Goth-black hair and flour-white faces were pressed against a wooden rail alongside a cloth albino rabbit with menacing pink eyes. Heather herself was angled limbs, lively gestures, constantly shifting expressions, touches of irony, and very quick intelligence. Designing a frame using Heather and her home was almost too easy, and was accompanied by the humbling awareness that her talent for representation was greater than mine.

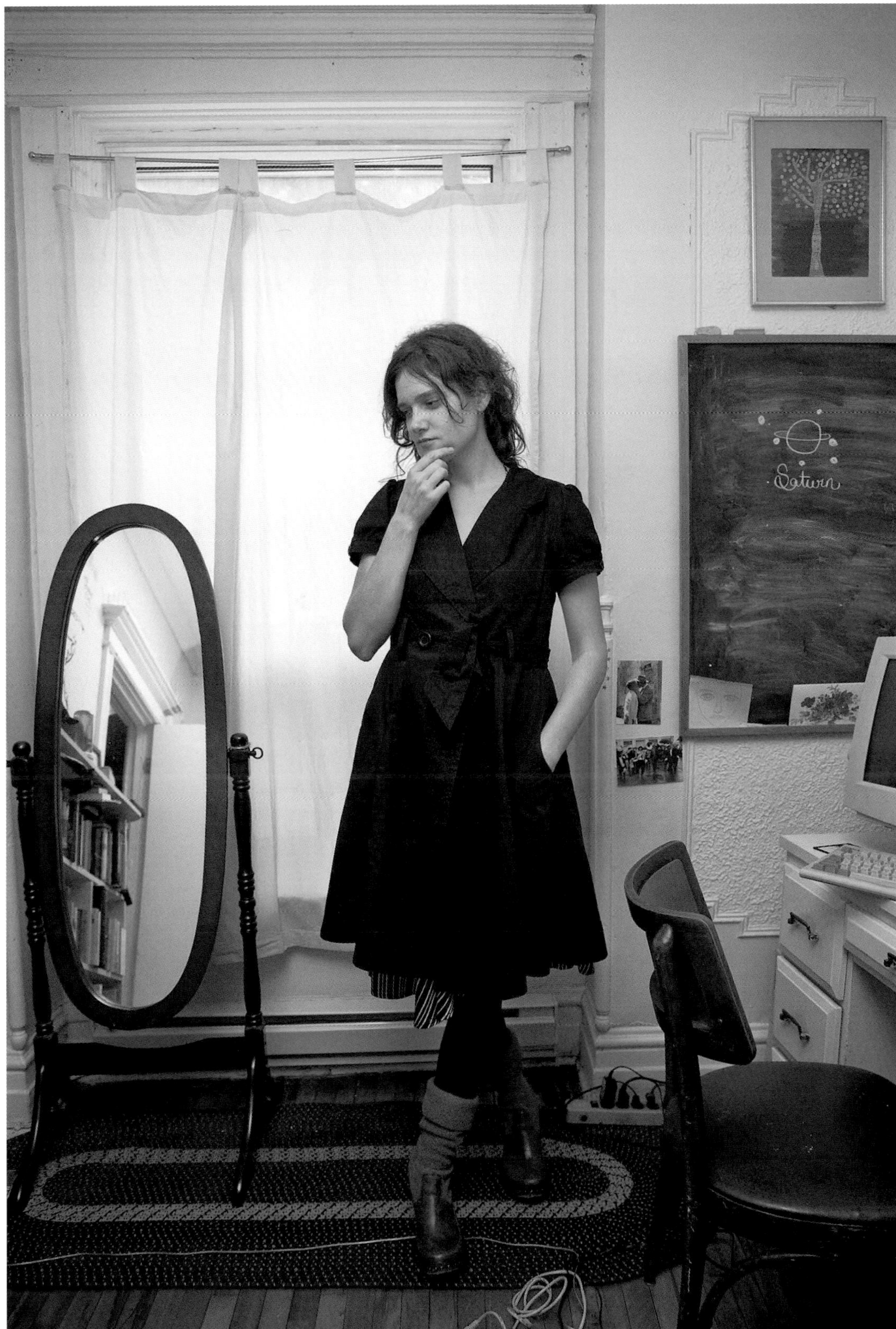
Saturn

YANN MARTEL IN PARC JEANNE-MANCE, PLATEAU MONT-ROYAL, SEPTEMBER 2001

YANN SHARED AN AIRY, high-ceilinged apartment overlooking the playing fields of a park. His roommates were other writers. Yann's room was austere. The advertising on wooden fruit crates that held a few books beside his bed provided the only colour. We talked about Montreal dance companies, spirituality, marriage, and the Camino Santiago de Compostela pilgrimage. He was fascinated by the idea of a pilgrim completing his long trek and burning even his clothes at the destination, being restored to the condition of a newborn. We left the apartment to shoot outside just as a light rain began. When Yann saw this image a few weeks later, he said, "I look a bit grim in that photo, don't you think? Isn't there one where I'm a little bit jollier?"

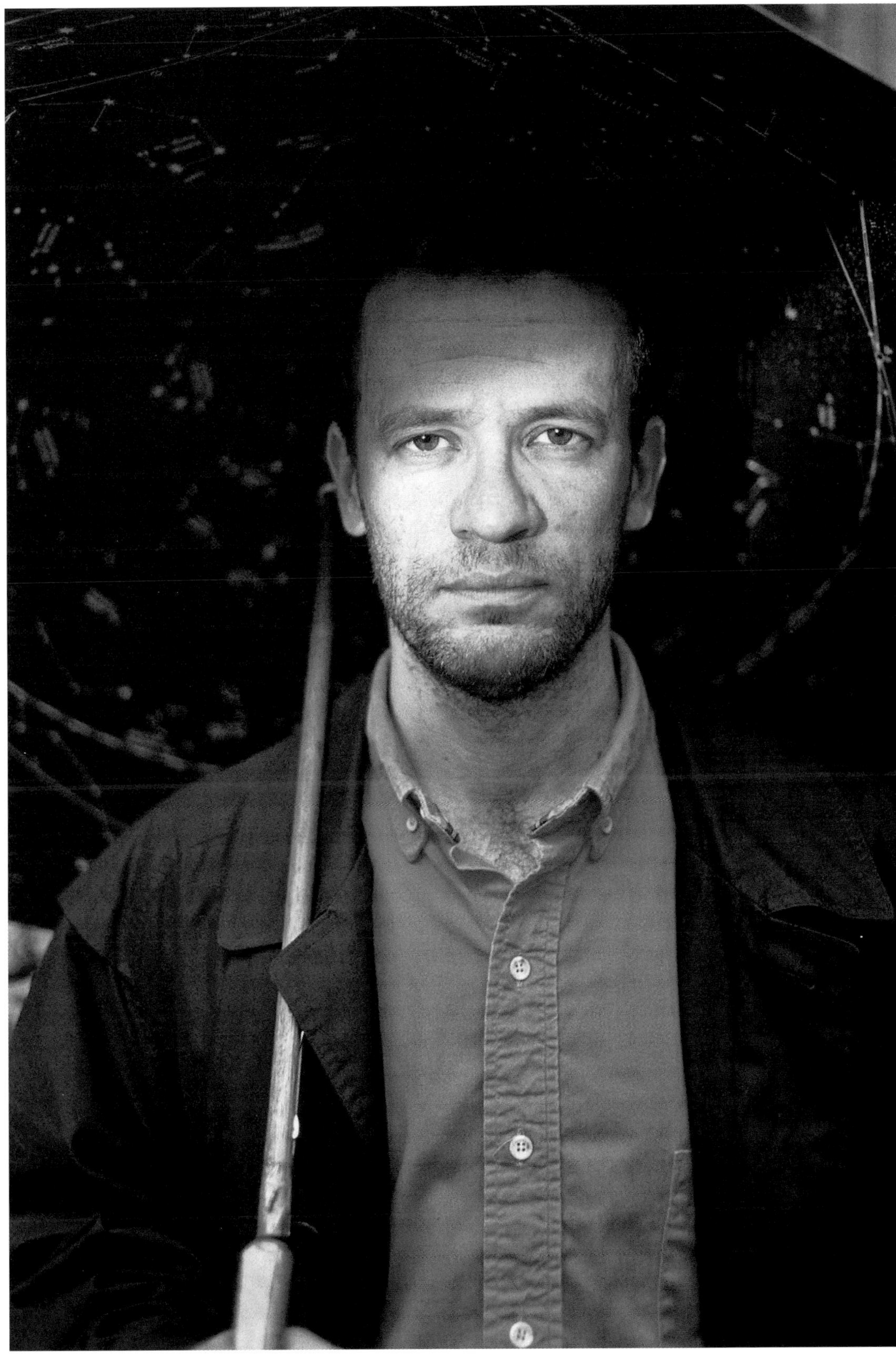

LOUIS DUDEK IN THE LIVING ROOM OF HIS HOME ON INGLESIDE AVENUE, WESTMOUNT, OCTOBER 2000

LOUIS DUDEK RECEIVED ME as he sat at the head of a long dining room table. He wore a necktie and four layers of clothing and he hovered over a chessboard, playing out both sides of a famous match from a book whose title was *Meet the Masters*. His manner toward me was teasing and a little prickly. He was testing both my knowledge and my intelligence. After he had relaxed, he told me that he was gravely ill and that keeping his spirits up was a battle. Then he sent me to his upstairs bathroom to look at a shower curtain printed with black and white publicity stills of movie stars from the nineteen-thirties and forties. "I've taken much comfort from that," he said. When I asked him if he would wrap it around himself for a photograph, to my astonishment, he agreed, but then decided his wife wouldn't like it. Toward the end of our meeting, all the energy left his body. "I'm just like Pierre Trudeau was," he said. "Waiting to die."

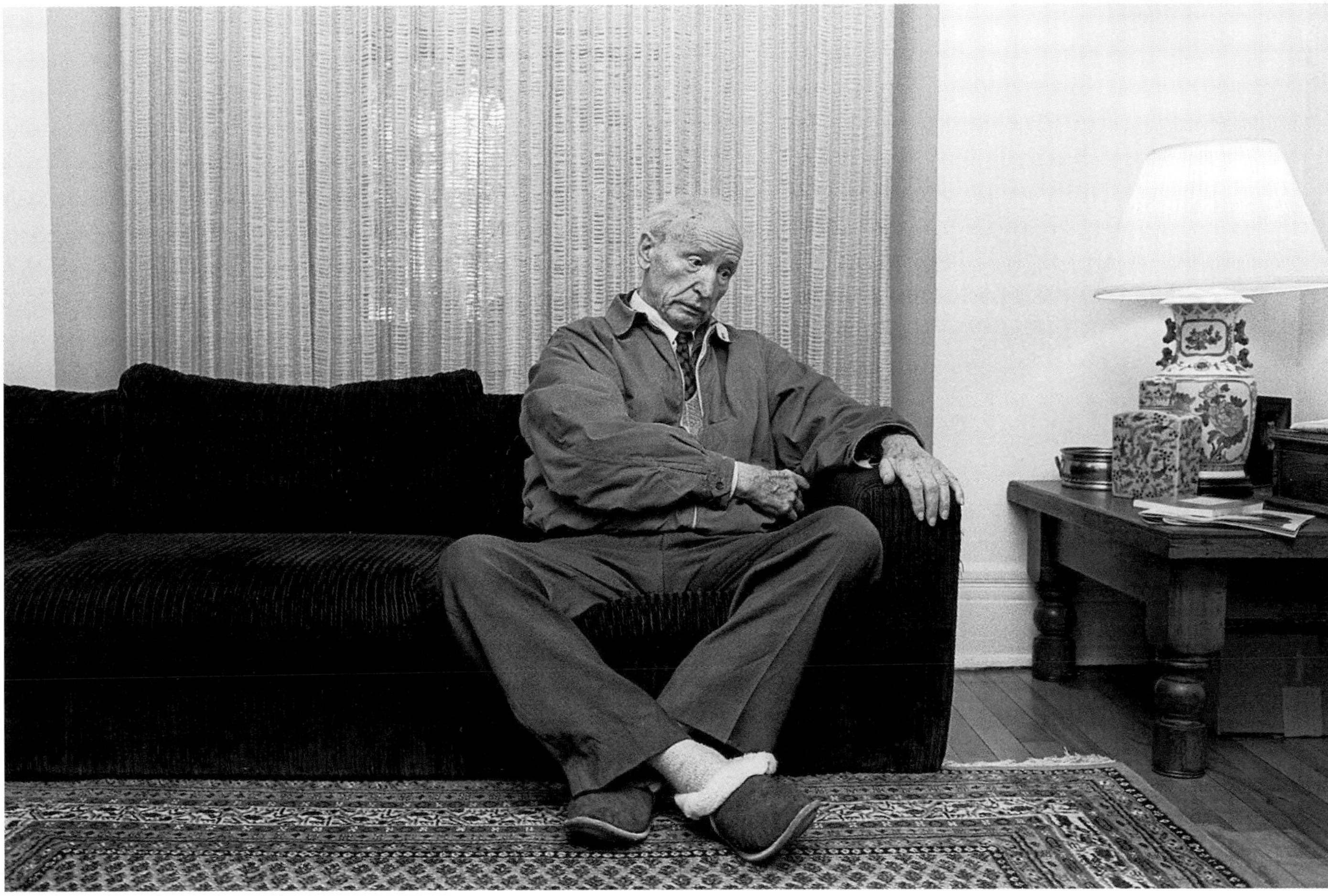

ERIN MOURÉ IN HER CONDOMINIUM ON RUE RACHEL, PLATEAU MONT-ROYAL, APRIL 2003

ERIN WAS WORKING ON TRANSLATIONS from Portuguese and Galician, including Chus Pato's *m-Tala*, when I visited her in her condo, a building that had in the past served as a youth hostel, a rectory, a nuns' residence, and a senior citizens' home. Two books, *This Sex Which Is Not One* and *Contos do Miño*, lay open on a chair beside her backpack. Another book, with a single hole through it, was displayed in a glass case made by a friend, a master cabinetmaker-artist. Faced with the even light, modernity, and neatness of her place, I began taking some artist-at-her-word-processor images in the hope that I could think of something better. At that point, Erin suddenly picked up an image of Elizabeth Taylor and gleefully held it over her own face. It was part of the collage she was working on for the *m-Tala* cover, which she described as "playing with notions of how women are seen and how/if they can speak."

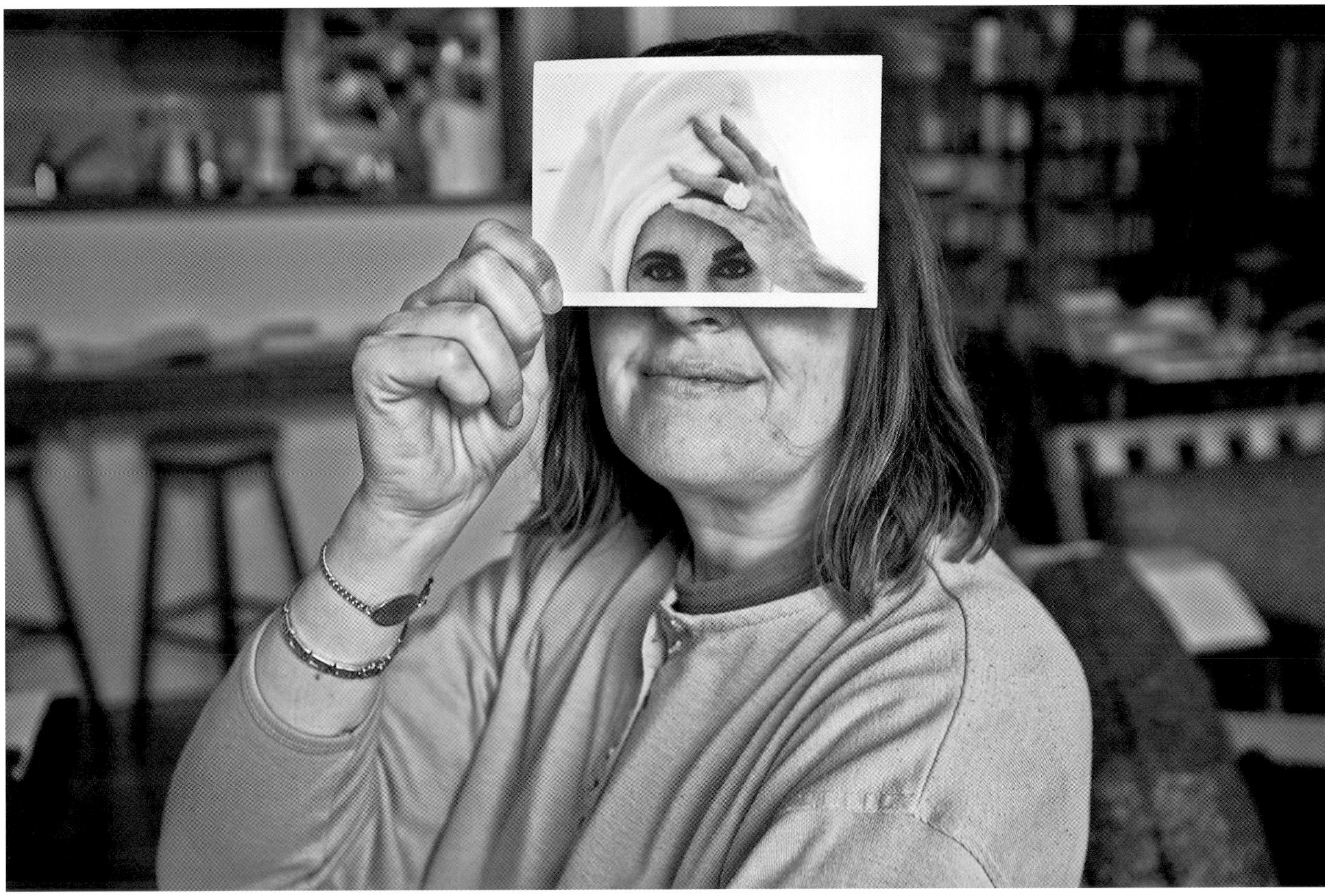

NEALE MCDEVITT ON HIS BASEMENT STAIRS,
STE-ANNE-DE-BELLEVUE, MARCH 2008

NEALE'S HOUSE HAD ONCE BEEN A FARM BUILDING that successive owners converted into a home by adding living space whenever and wherever they needed it. Consequently, many of its neat little rooms felt like parts of different houses. Neale had just had the chilly, rock-walled crawl space under the house sprayed with insulating foam, and was showing it to me. As we climbed up and down through the history of the house, he told me a story. He had once been a member of the Canadian weight lifting team, and still rose a little after 4 A.M. each day so that he could lift weights before going to work. Trying to beat a drug test, he told me, the members of his team had once collected steroid-free urine from their trainer. Then they used a catheter to transfer it through their penises to their bladders. When I wondered out loud why he hadn't written about life in that world, he shrugged helplessly, as though he hadn't yet been able to answer that question for himself.

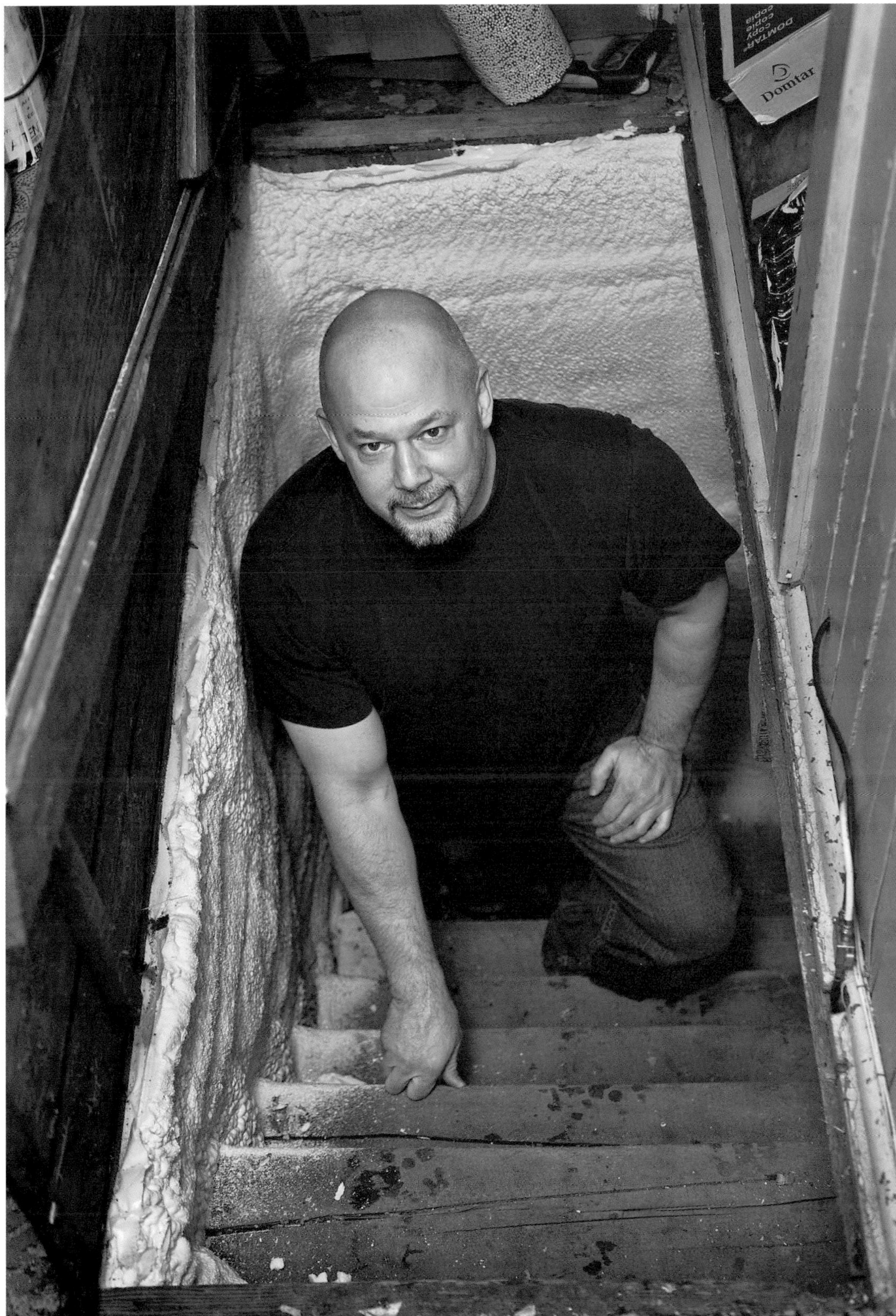
Domtar

Elyse Gasco in a coffee shop
on Boulevard St-Laurent, Plateau Mont-Royal, February 2000

Whenever I called, Elyse Gasco's answering machine played the sound of a howling wolf. My messages were never returned. Someone suggested that a call to her husband, a veterinarian, might produce a contact. Finally, we met when she was being interviewed for a literary magazine. I was struck by her slimness and pale skin, which made her eyes look disconcertingly large. Her expression was wan and her manner seemingly indifferent. Some time later, by chance, I met Elyse on the street, where she told me that writing had taken a back seat in her life to child-rearing. "I looked so gaunt when you took your pictures because I had pneumonia!" she explained, then added "Bye!" and quite literally skipped away.

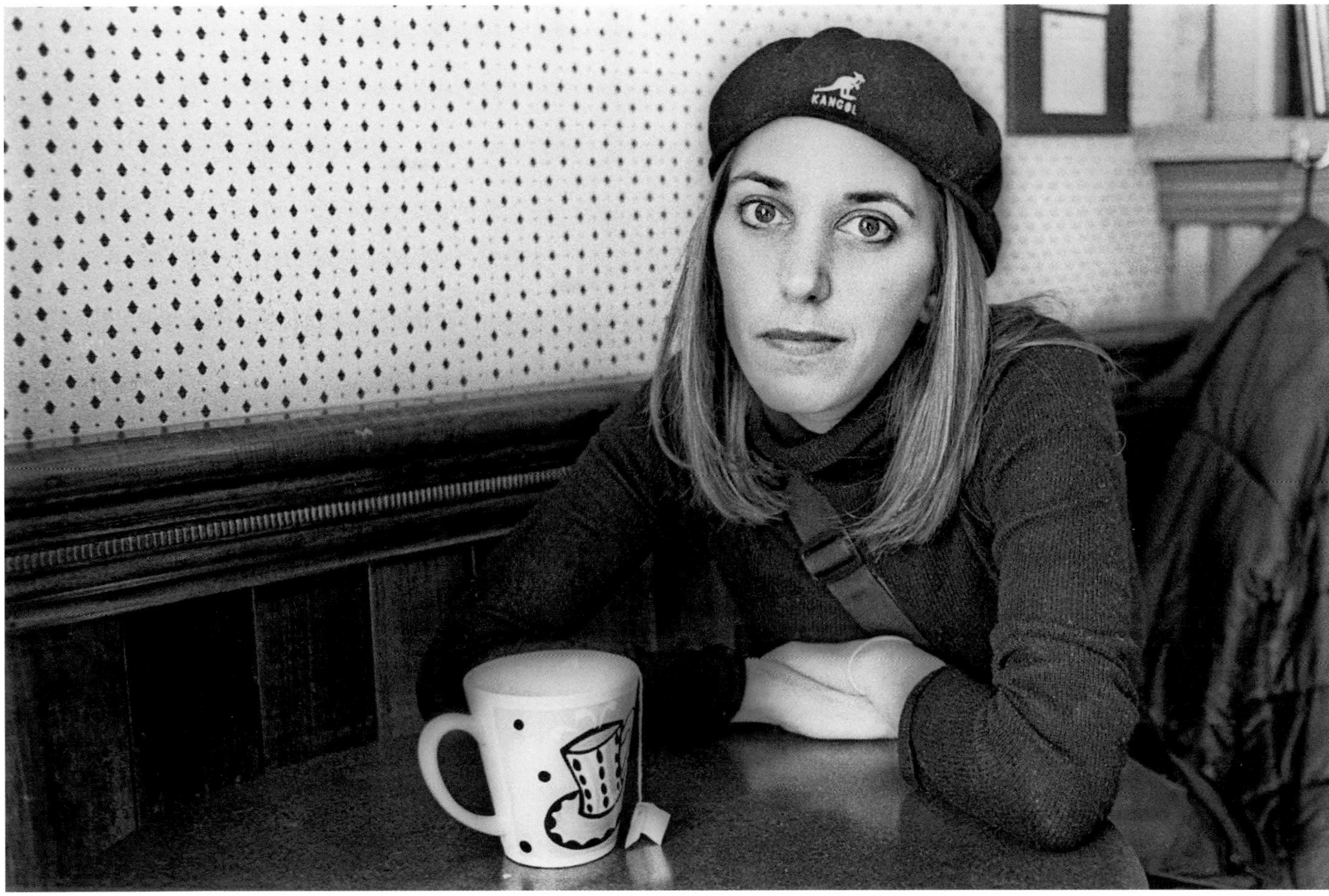
KANGOL

PETER BEHRENS IN AN UNDERGROUND PARKING GARAGE, RUE MACKAY, MONTREAL, OCTOBER 1999

PETER WAS ON THE ROAD. He seemed always to be on the road; it was his home as much as anywhere. His first published book was titled *Night Driving*. Once, when he worked as a Hollywood scriptwriter, I saw him step out of his car on a visit to Montreal wearing a white duster and stride along the sidewalk like a character from Walter Hill's movie *The Long Riders*. We met this day in a Czech coffee shop to talk and, over apricot *kolaches*, I learned about his wife's new documentary film, his work on an indie Canadian film, the recent projects of his old friend and mentor, the writer Clark Blaise, and his plans for a novel about Irish immigrants to Canada. That novel became *The Law of Dreams* and won the Governor General's Award several years later. Peter once wrote, "The law of dreams is, keep moving." Even sitting face to face with Peter and photographing him, it was always hard to escape the feeling that he was distracted, engaged elsewhere, endlessly travelling in his thoughts.

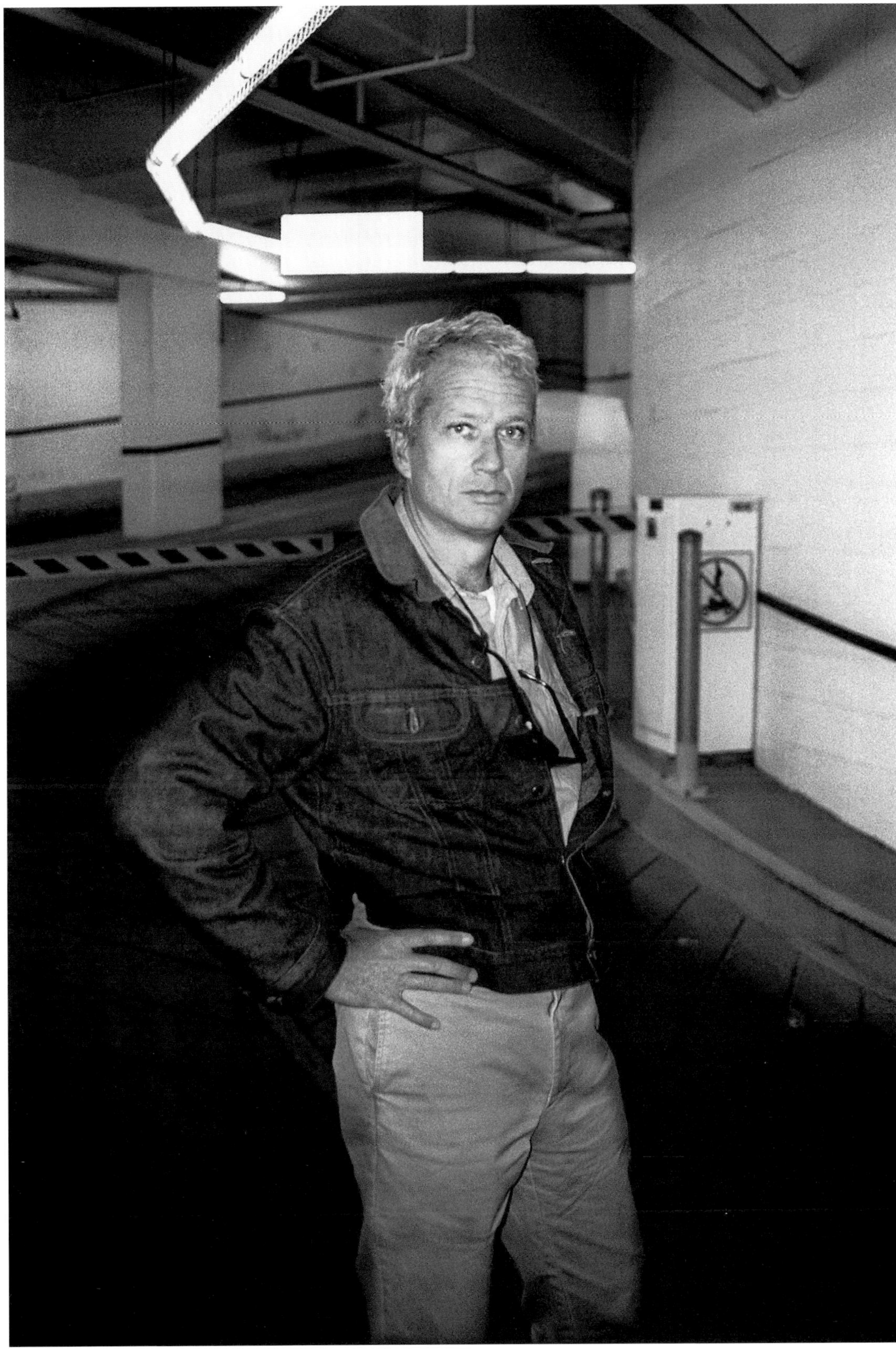

Connie Barnes Rose in her dining room, Outremont, April 2008

Connie's first book was a collection of unflinchingly realistic stories set in a small Nova Scotia town singularly like her own home town. Shortly after our portrait session began, she told me a rather terrifying story—which she acted out with physical energy and pleasure in the telling—of the time her daughter encountered a burglar in their Outremont home while Connie, ignorant of what was happening, waited outside in her car. After telling the story, she admitted that she had been aware of playing a role for my camera, that she was at once inside the story she was narrating and aware that its performance gave her a way to present herself. In that, there is a parallel with the writer whose fiction is autobiographical, and who, to write a story, is in constant negotiation with memory, truthfulness, display, and invention. The painting behind Connie is by her friend Judith Berry.

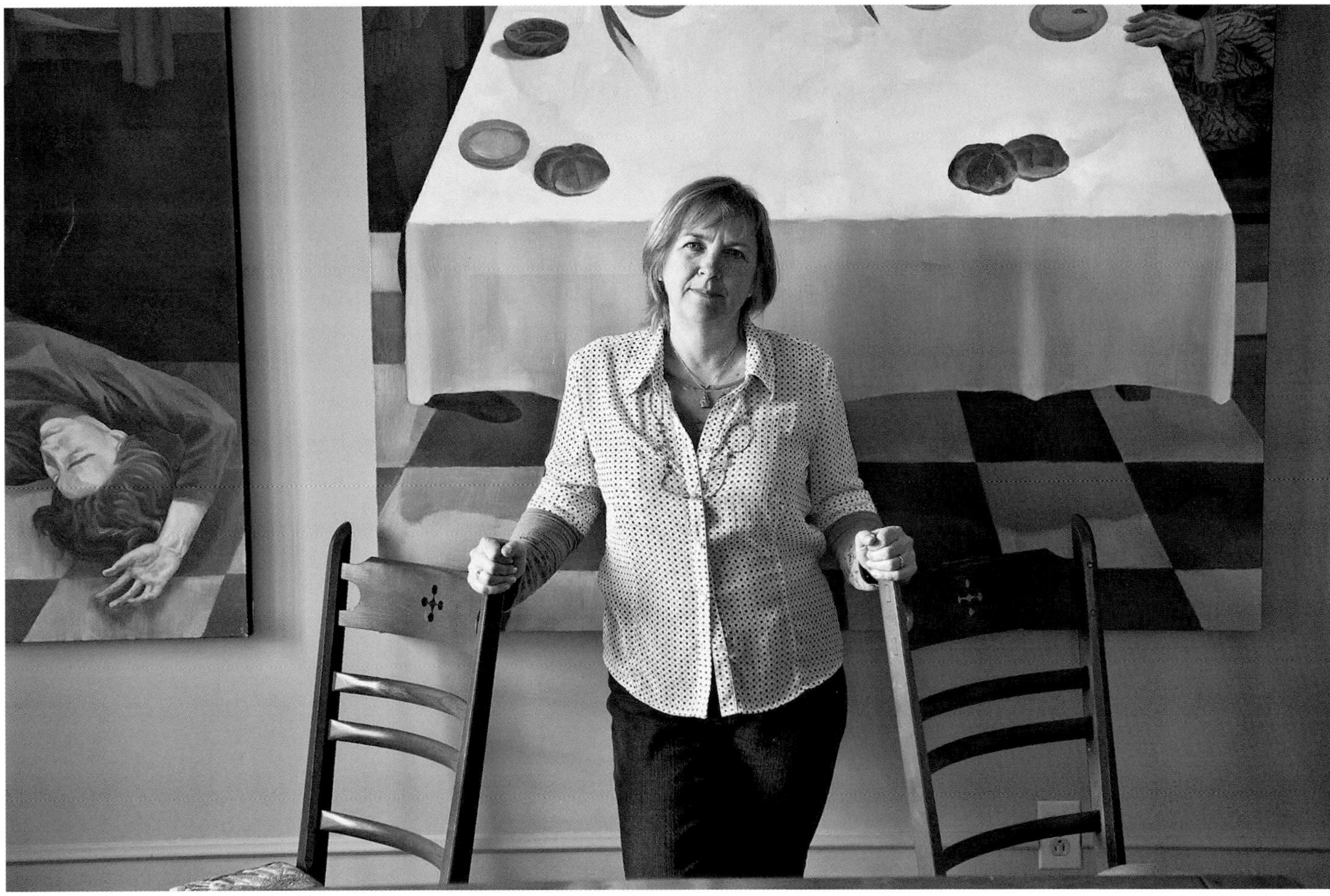

Steve Luxton in his shared apartment on avenue de l'Esplanade, Plateau Mont-Royal, March 2005

STEVE LIVED IN AN APARTMENT whose lofty ceiling, plaster medallions, oak rosettes, and typical Montreal *double salon* were shared with two other writers, both of whom I had also photographed. When I stepped in, Steve was lying on a couch and reading Jacques Barzun's *From Dawn to Decadence: 500 Years of Western Cultural Life*, which he enthusiastically recommended. The even light, deep shadows, and elegantly detailed *fin-de-siècle* plaster work in the apartment all argued for a shot of conventional literary seriousness, and I took many. Steve, always theatrical when called on, changed the mood by clambering onto a tree-trunk coffee table to recite his poetry. Later, he was anxious to show me an amateur recording made of Bob Dylan in a Montreal coffeehouse in the early sixties. He handled the CD as though it were a delicate piece of ancient pottery, putting it down only to pick up a mouth harp and blow into it with triumphant, bluesy force.

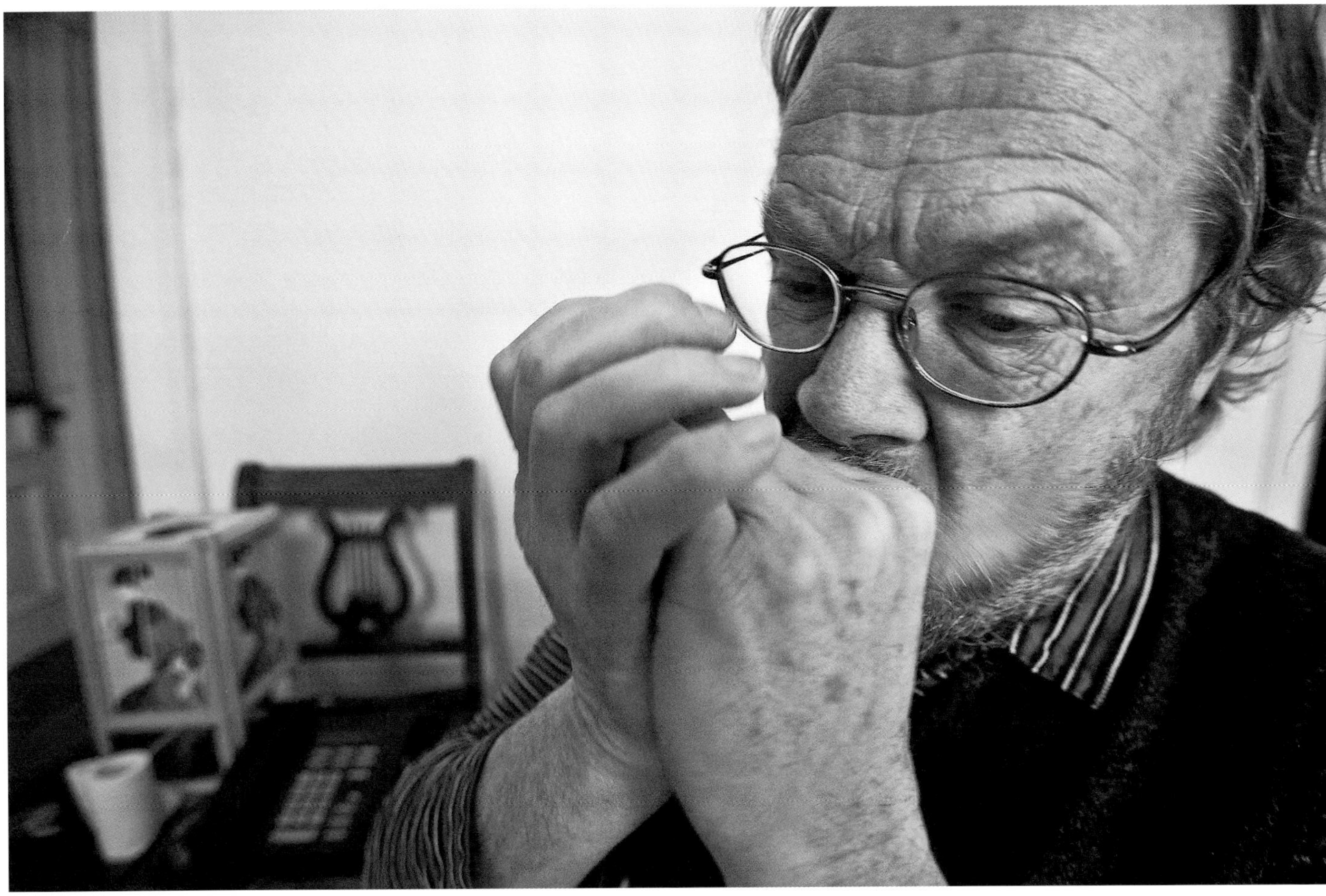

Anne Carson in her apartment
on avenue de l'Esplanade, Plateau Mont-Royal, October 1998

BEFORE OUR SESSION BEGAN, Anne showed me her paintings of South American volcanoes and laughed at their limited palettes, explaining that she had only had three or four colours of paint with her when she painted them. The colours were fine for volcanoes, but must have posed a challenge for her llamas. A drawing she had made of Gertrude Stein oversaw our relaxed discussion of art, her map of ancient Greece, and her family's summer cabin in Ontario. After a while, I suggested that we start taking pictures. Anne agreed readily, then paused indecisively for a moment, and told me about the distress a recent portrait session for *The New York Times* had caused her. Then she placed a surprising restriction on our shoot: "You can only take one picture of my face," she said. It was stated in such a matter-of-fact way that it sounded almost like an ordinary limitation. When her running-shoed feet went briefly *en pointe*, the one picture was made.

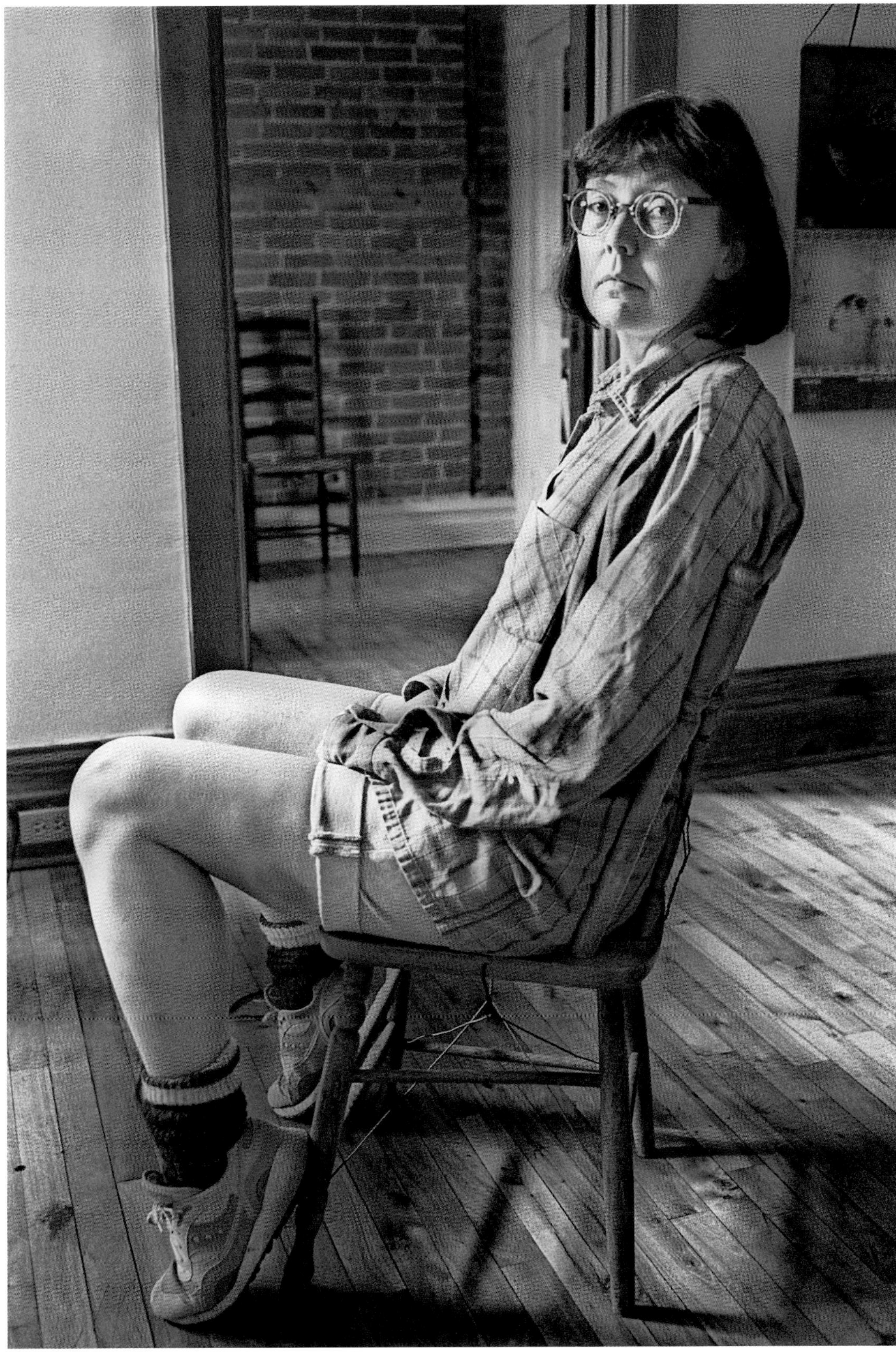

Jason Camlot in a stairwell of the "fur building" on rue Ste-Catherine, Montreal, April 2000

THE SO-CALLED FUR BUILDING is one of three such buildings that have been the centres of the fur industry in Montreal. This one's proper name is the Belgo Building. When I told Jason that the photographs were to be made in a setting where the writer lived, worked, or played, he suggested the place where his father worked in the fur industry, and where Jason himself had begun to learn the trade of cutting and matching fur. Lately, though, the Belgo had begun a slow transition from pelts to art, offering spaces for galleries and dance studios. Nevertheless, Jason still roamed the floors and stairwells as though it were as familiar as a home. We stopped to look out huge windows whose frames were thick with ancient paint that curled like wood shavings. I asked Jason to sit on a radiator under one of these windows and he did so, waiting while I fiddled with my camera. After a minute, he grimaced inexplicably and asked if I was about ready. It was only then that I noticed that the radiator was almost too hot to touch. As we were leaving the building, late in the day, small balls of fur blew before us down the long wooden hallway like tumbleweeds in a western movie.

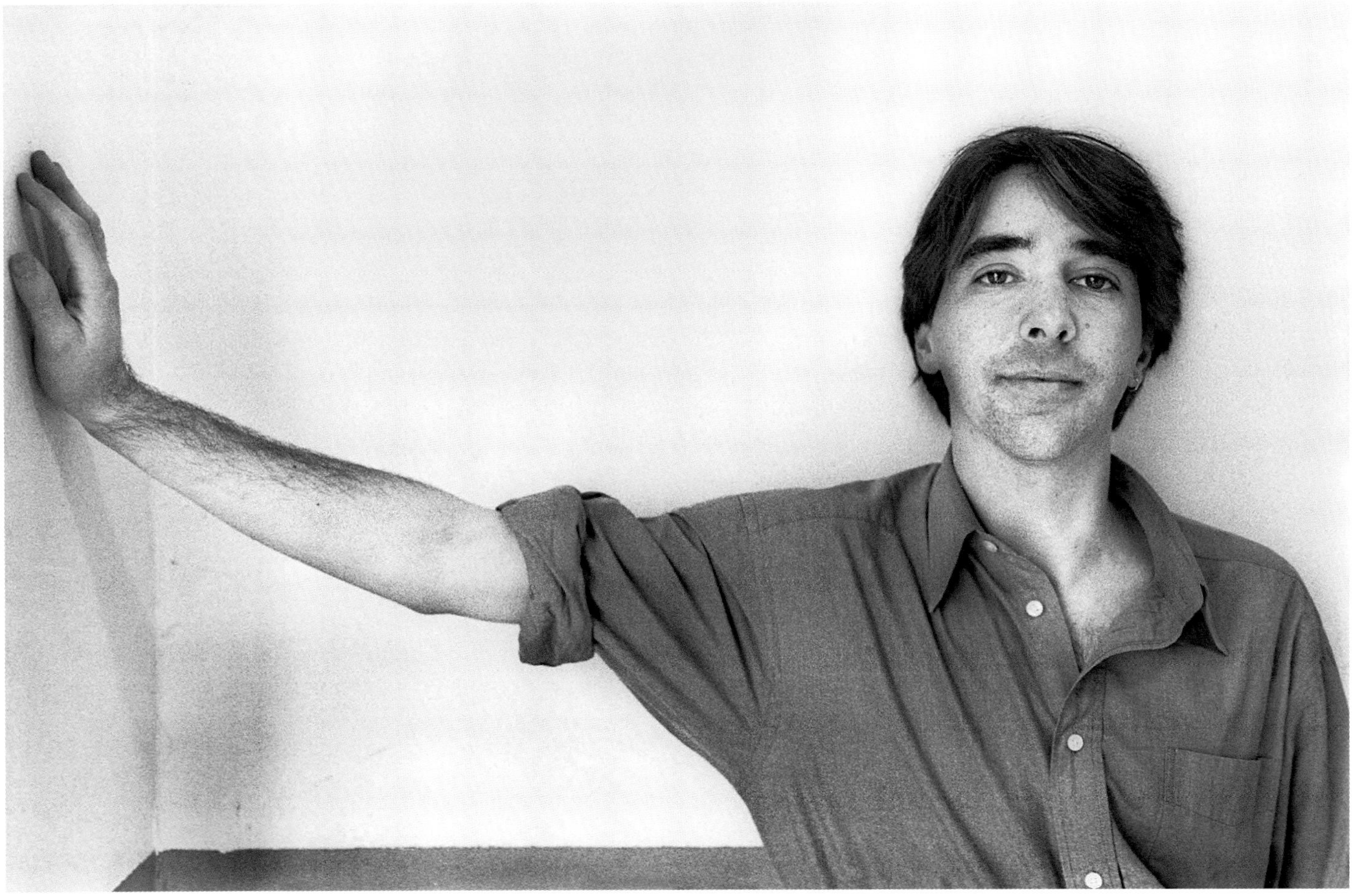

Eric Ormsby in his living room in Habitat 67
ON MONTREAL HARBOUR, FEBRUARY 2001

ERIC ORMSBY LIVED IN HABITAT, the radical housing design by Moshe Safdie that was opened during Expo 67. It was a particularly cold day when I visited him and Habitat, a jumble of pre-cast concrete boxes with exterior entrances, faced the wind whistling off the St. Lawrence River and the Old Port. When I arrived, my shoulders shook with the cold and it took me a moment to get my bearings, physically and socially. Eric invited me in and briefly introduced me to a jeans-clad woman with an eastern European accent. She was cleaning the kitchen and glanced up briefly to say hello before she returned to her work. I thought he said she was the housekeeper. When we sat down to talk, the woman came to sit close to Eric and affectionately took his arm. It wasn't until days later that I discovered the "housekeeper" was his wife, Irena Murray, Chief Curator of Rare Books and Special Collections at McGill University. Eric's worried expression may have mirrored my own perplexity about the nature of his domestic arrangements.

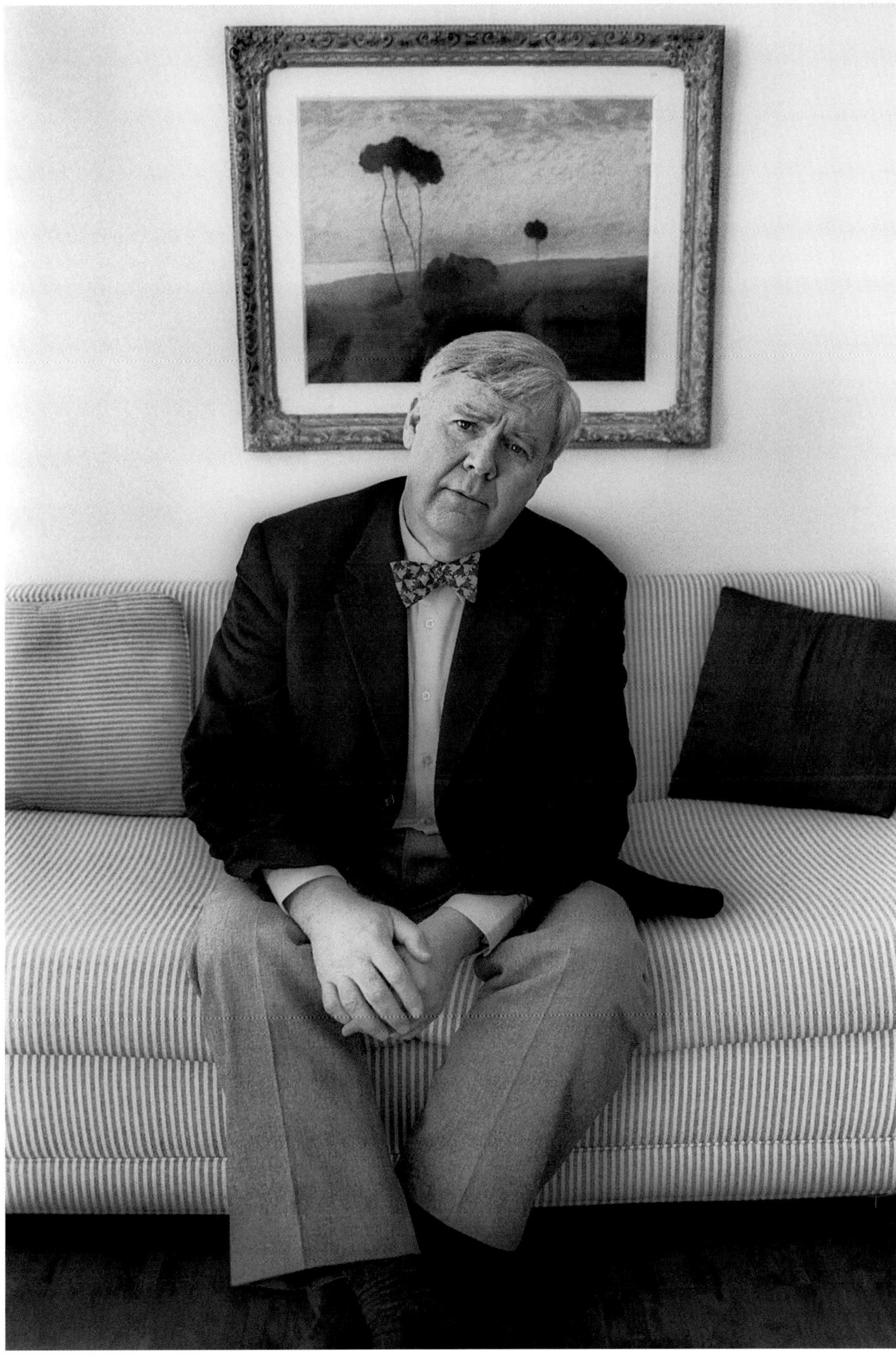

VITTORIO ROSSI IN THE BASEMENT OF HIS HOUSE, VILLE ST-PIERRE, FEBRUARY 2008

A YOUNG MAN I DIDN'T KNOW came to the front door of Vittorio's building, called loudly for him, and disappeared without glancing back at me. Vittorio's door then opened and he greeted me warmly, explaining that, after the death of his parents, he had moved into the small family home in this suburb of apartment buildings, duplexes, and boxy houses a few métro stops outside the border of Montreal. His sister, he said, lived upstairs. It was a home his father, a carpenter whose portrait revealed the well-defined, masculine features of a forties movie star, had built. Vittorio was proud of his father's work and tried to replicate its quality in his own renovations. After telling me that he was developing a television series about Montreal's mob connections with the American mafia, he took me to the basement. There he showed me the remnants of a "second kitchen," where everyone in his family would gather to eat. At that moment, his arms spread to encompass a departed past. Now, the principle activity in the basement is his writing, where he sits at a custom-built work station surrounded by movie posters, literature, and manuals on screenwriting.

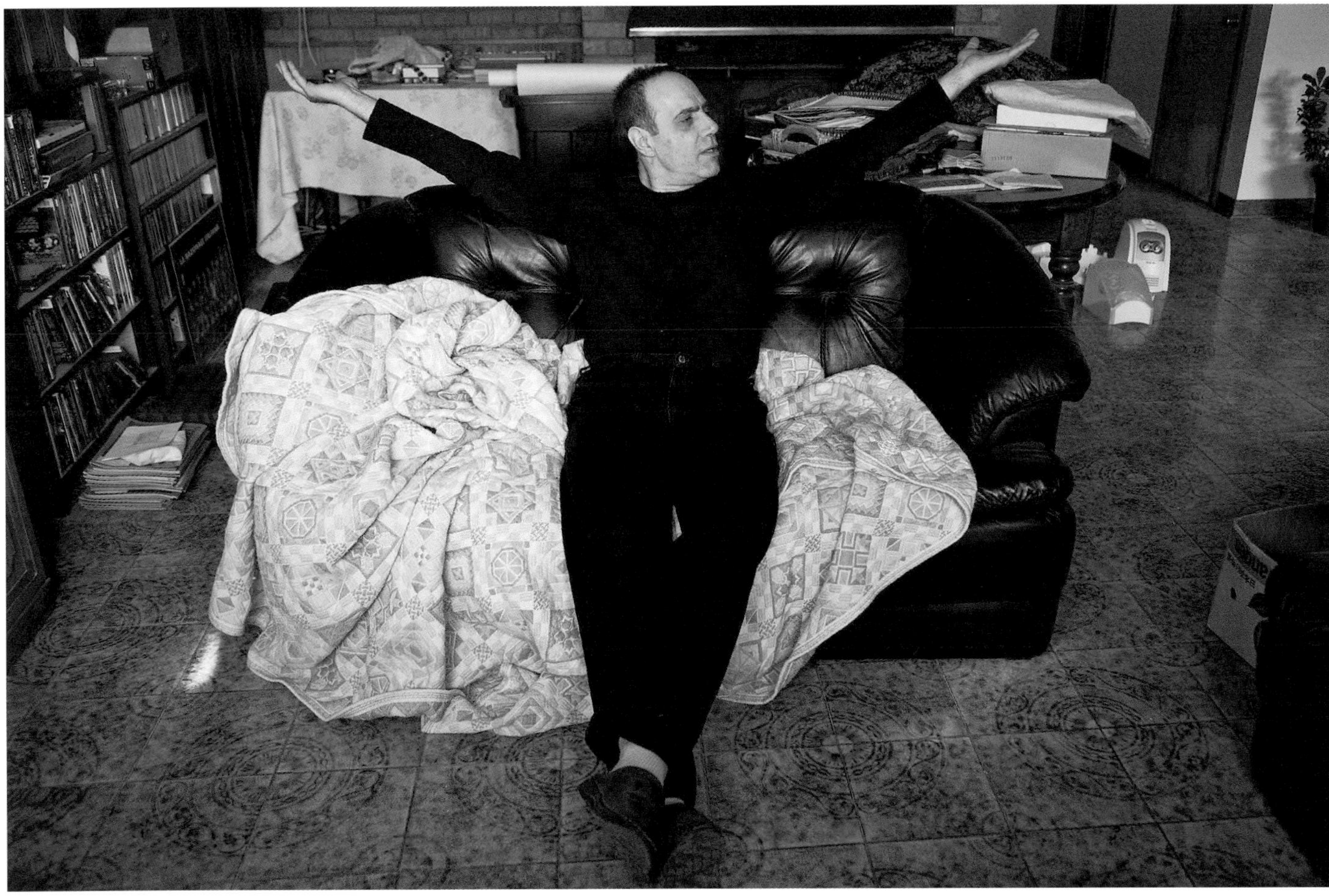

David Fennario in the doorway
to his Plateau Mont-Royal studio, August 1999

DAVID FENNARIO LIVED in a working-class bedroom community, Verdun, on the southwest flank of the city of Montreal, but I met him outside a trendy café on Boulevard St-Laurent, where he was offering copies of *Socialist Worker* and *Socialisme International* to people passing on the street. From there, we walked east to his cramped studio in a house that had been divided into residential and office spaces. On the sidewalk in front of the house, someone had written *"Vive le Québec libre!"* in thick blue chalk. Inside the studio, a yard of bookshelf bent under the weight of books on the JFK assassination and the subsequent conspiracy theories. David fondly showed me a desk that had been given to his father when he was working in the home of a wealthy family. David's own political sentiments were populist and communist, fueled by the experience of having grown up resentful and poor on "the avenues" in Verdun, but his attachment to the desk—an upper-class castoff—was untouched by irony. He was a strange, non-coercive communist, and, as a photographic subject, even his movements and posture were fluid and haphazard.

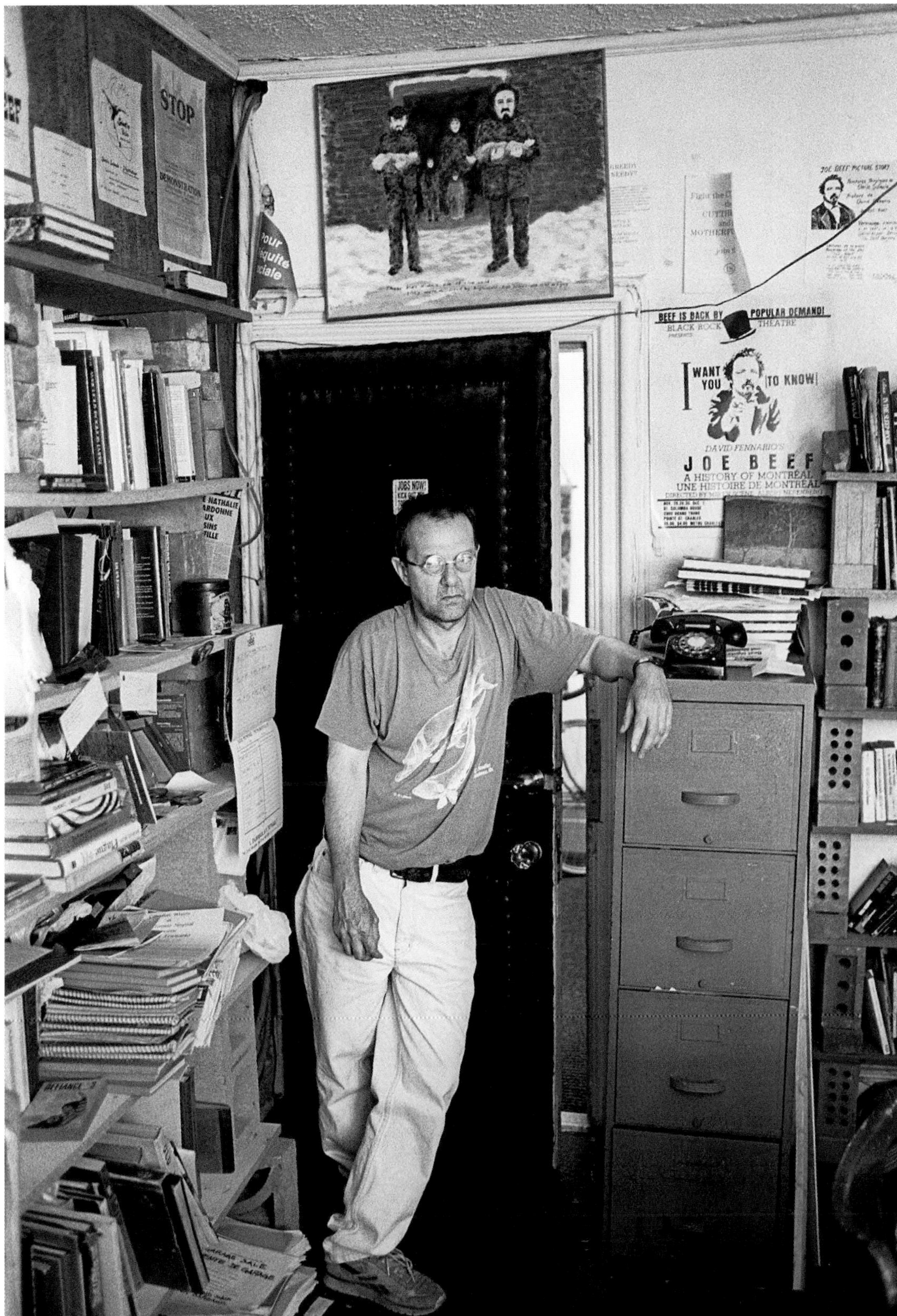
STOP
DEMONSTRATION
BEEF IS BACK BY POPULAR DEMAND!
BLACK ROCK
THEATRE
I WANT YOU TO KNOW!
DAVID FENNARIO'S
JOE BEEF
A HISTORY OF MONTREAL
UNE HISTOIRE DE MONTREAL
JOBS NOW!

DIMITRI NASRALLAH AT HIS FRONT DOOR,

RUE COURSOL, LITTLE BURGUNDY, JANUARY 2006

IT WAS A FRIGHTFULLY COLD DAY, and Dimitri and I were delaying leaving his basement flat, where he lived with his partner, a painter. The flat was a long, minimalist tunnel a few steps down from a pretty street undergoing gentrification. It was also a few blocks away from the historic, crumbling Negro Community Centre, and a short walk from the Atwater Market and his two favourite lunch restaurants, Green Spot and La Belle Province. We talked about recent Lebanese history, Dimitri's somewhat anxious wait for a grant that would finance the South American travel necessary for research on his next novel, the part-time job he had assembling a literary database, and lunch. When we finally stepped outside and walked along the railway tracks bordering the Lachine Canal, my fingers quickly lost sensation in the cold and I couldn't even feel the shutter button. We wound up at Green Spot in St-Henri, where a cheery waitress, sensitive to the expectations of a regular, immediately brought Dimitri two large hot dogs with enough chopped onions piled on them to have burned a hole through the stomach of someone less vigorous than he was.

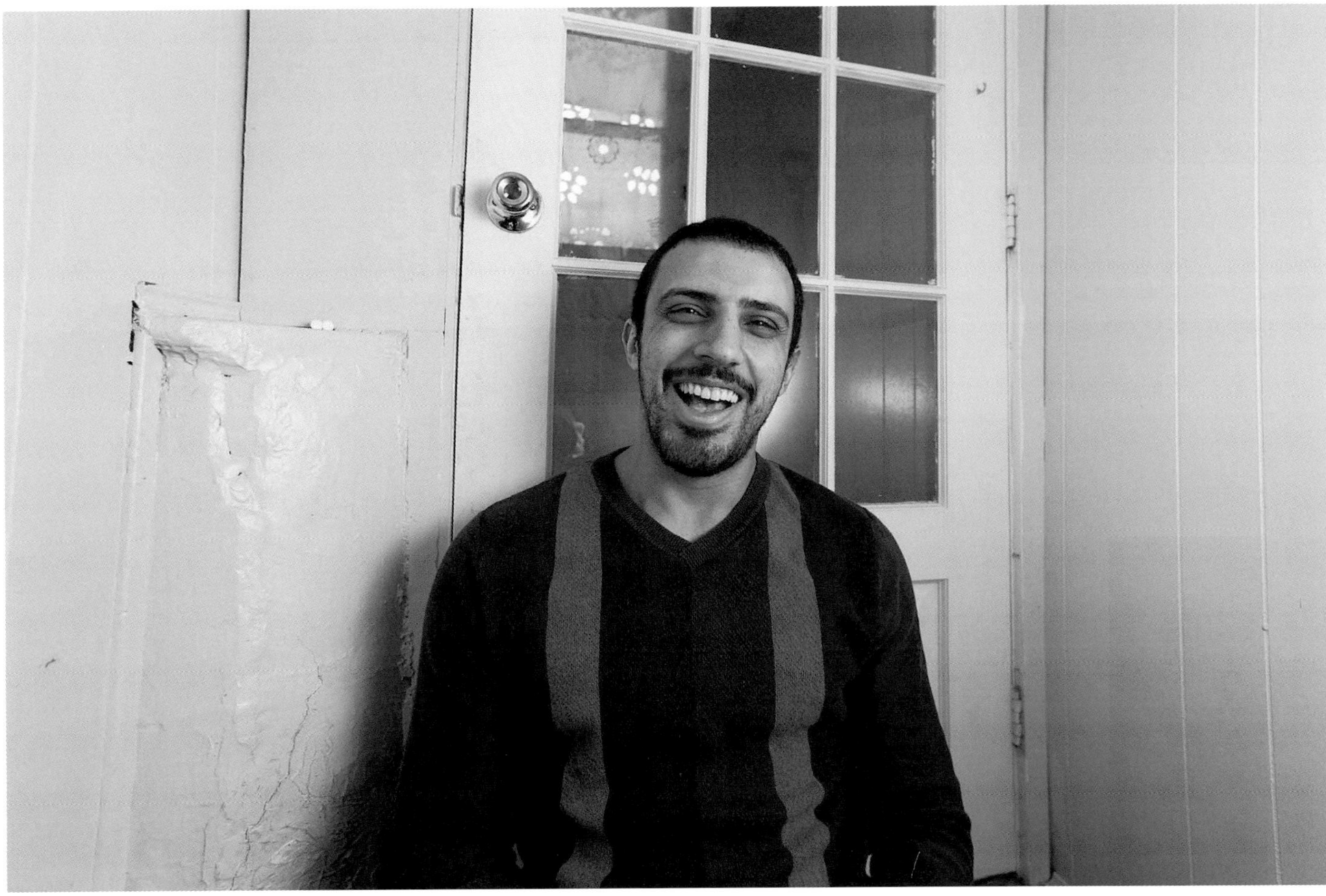

Michael Harris in his dining room, lower Westmount, August 1999

Michael's house was filled with art, including a large portrait of him by the painter Marion Wagschal. In the painting, he wore only a military raincoat and slumped carelessly in an armchair with his legs stretched out before him. Ordinarily, Michael looked poised, either for physical movement or, his left eyebrow slightly raised, for judgment. Despite his appearance of calculated self-possession, he was an easygoing subject who let me photograph him throughout his house. When I followed him to an upstairs guest room, he sat on the bed, looked at me pointedly, and said that this was the room where he let a friend—a well-known writer whom he named—bring his mistress. It was hard to tell if this was a small test of my composure or merely a fact about this part of his house. Michael's curious alertness and desire to challenge were absent in the Wagschal painting but are evident in every photograph I took.

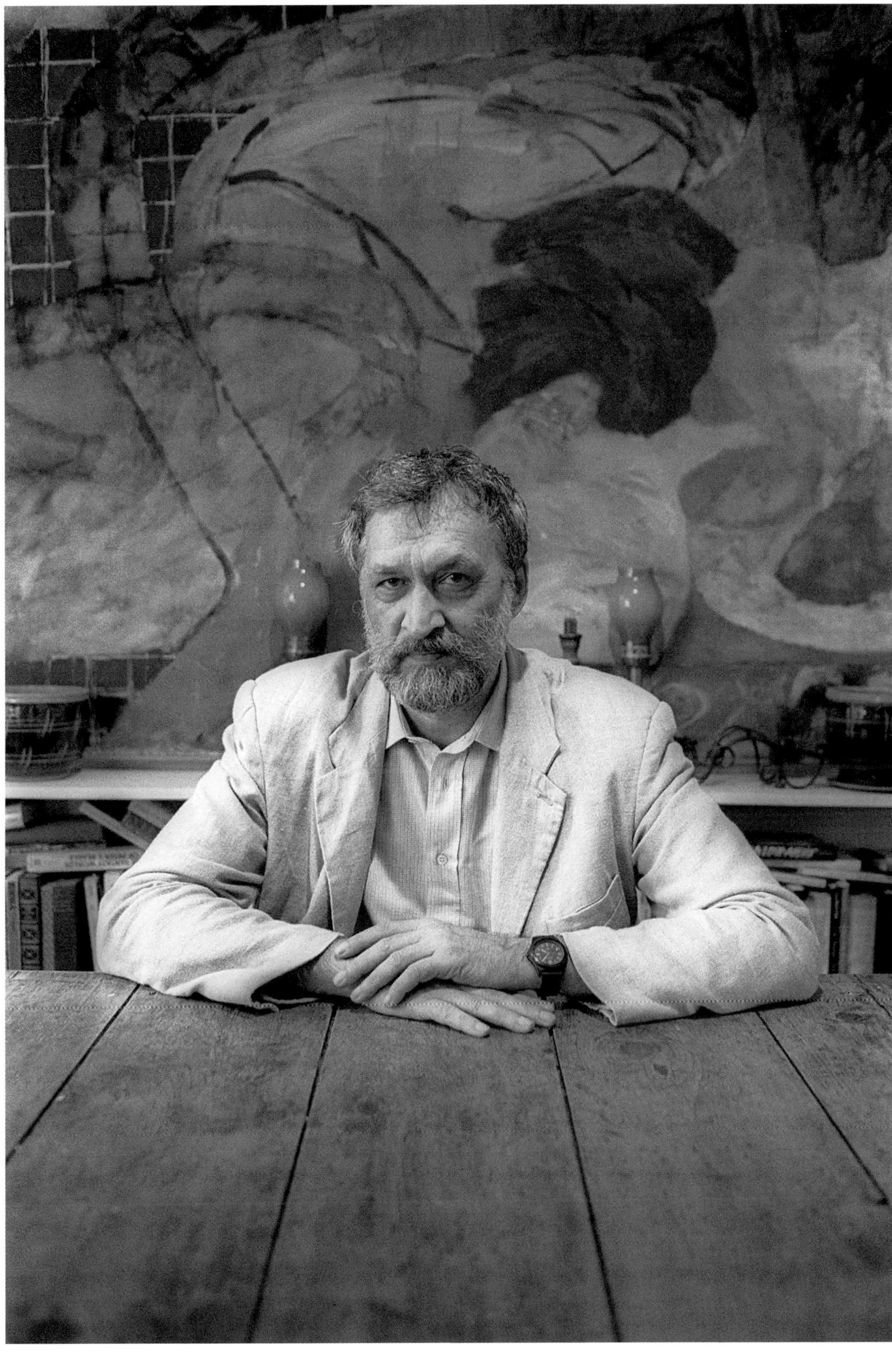

SHEILA FISCHMAN UPSTAIRS IN HER HOME ON RUE CLARK, PLATEAU MONT-ROYAL, DECEMBER 2007

SHEILA FISCHMAN HAD CANCELLED our originally scheduled shoot, with sincere apologies, because of the death of a close family member. I was immediately struck by the modesty and lack of a sense of entitlement in her manner. That impression was confirmed when I arrived at her home, a handsomely renovated building that had been workers' housing around the turn of the last century. Sheila made no particular demands about the ways I could photograph her and was at ease with the camera. We also talked easily—about the past and about the accommodations one makes with it, and about the inevitable future. Our conversation, despite being tinged with a sad consciousness of mortality, was a lively one. Before I left, we stepped into her kitchen and she showed me some strips of candied grapefruit peel that she was trying to make, based on her girlhood memories of her mother's recipe.

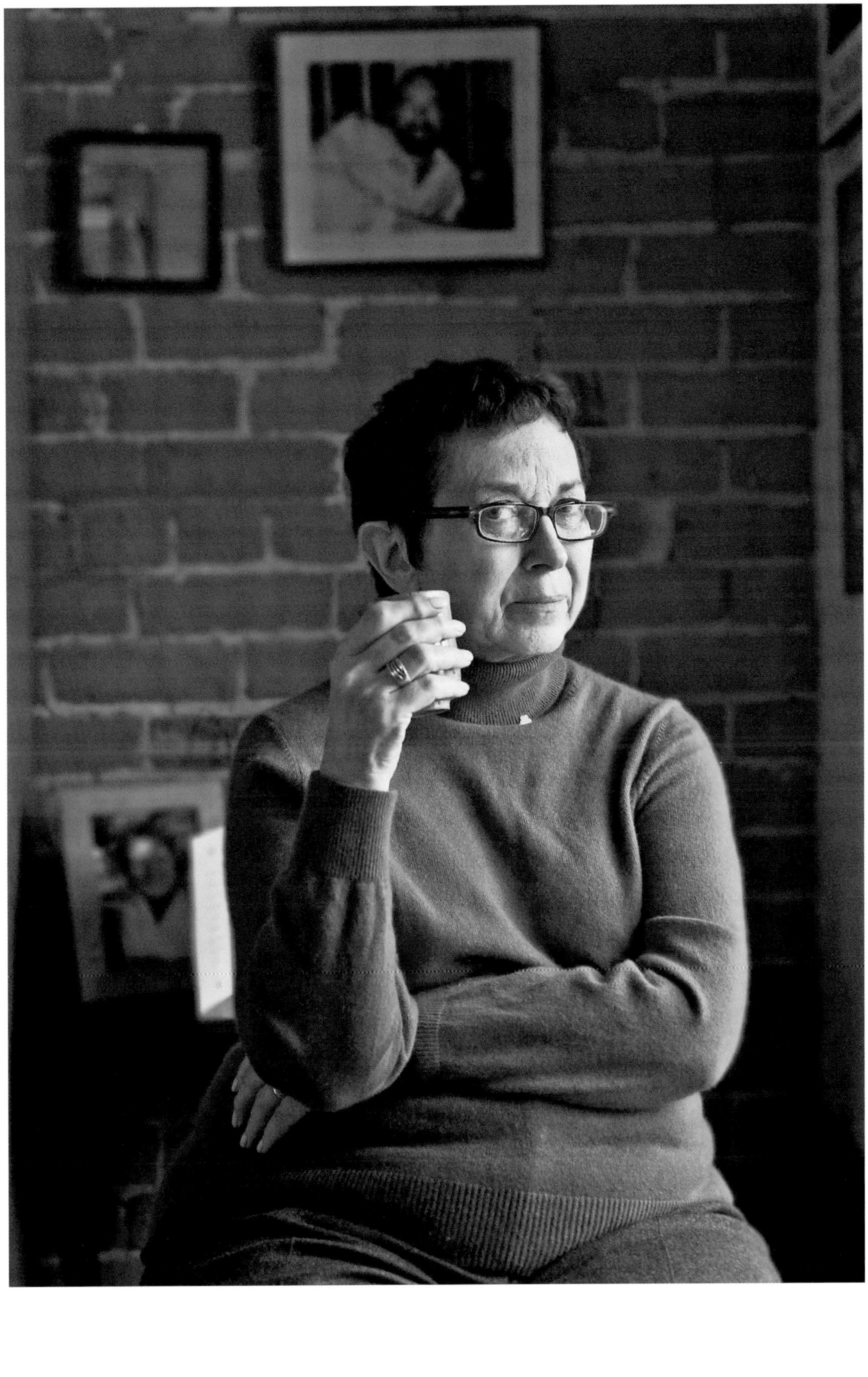

WILL AITKEN UPSTAIRS IN HIS HOME,
RUE DE LA ROCHE, PLATEAU MONT-ROYAL, FEBRUARY 2008

WILL AITKEN MET ME AT THE DOOR and apologetically declared that he had a hangover. Then he collected a new puppy that was very anxious to join our shoot, and ushered me in. The apartment, which he owned, was a combination of rough and rehabilitated, with an iron staircase circling in front of a pitted stucco wall and a hanging sculpture by his friend Anne Carson, the poet. The very long and chilly white room at the top of the stairs overlooked snowy rooftops. As we worked, Will judiciously encouraged me to speak about the experience of photographing Anne Carson. I was sure he was evaluating my discretion and my judgment, and being protective of his friend, which made me hesitant to speak. When we exhausted the visual possibilities of the white room, we descended the iron staircase, passing some campy personal treasures that had survived a fire in his building. These included a painted dog that was more accommodating than the new puppy, which bit the hem of my pants leg and shook it violently as I followed Will from location to location.

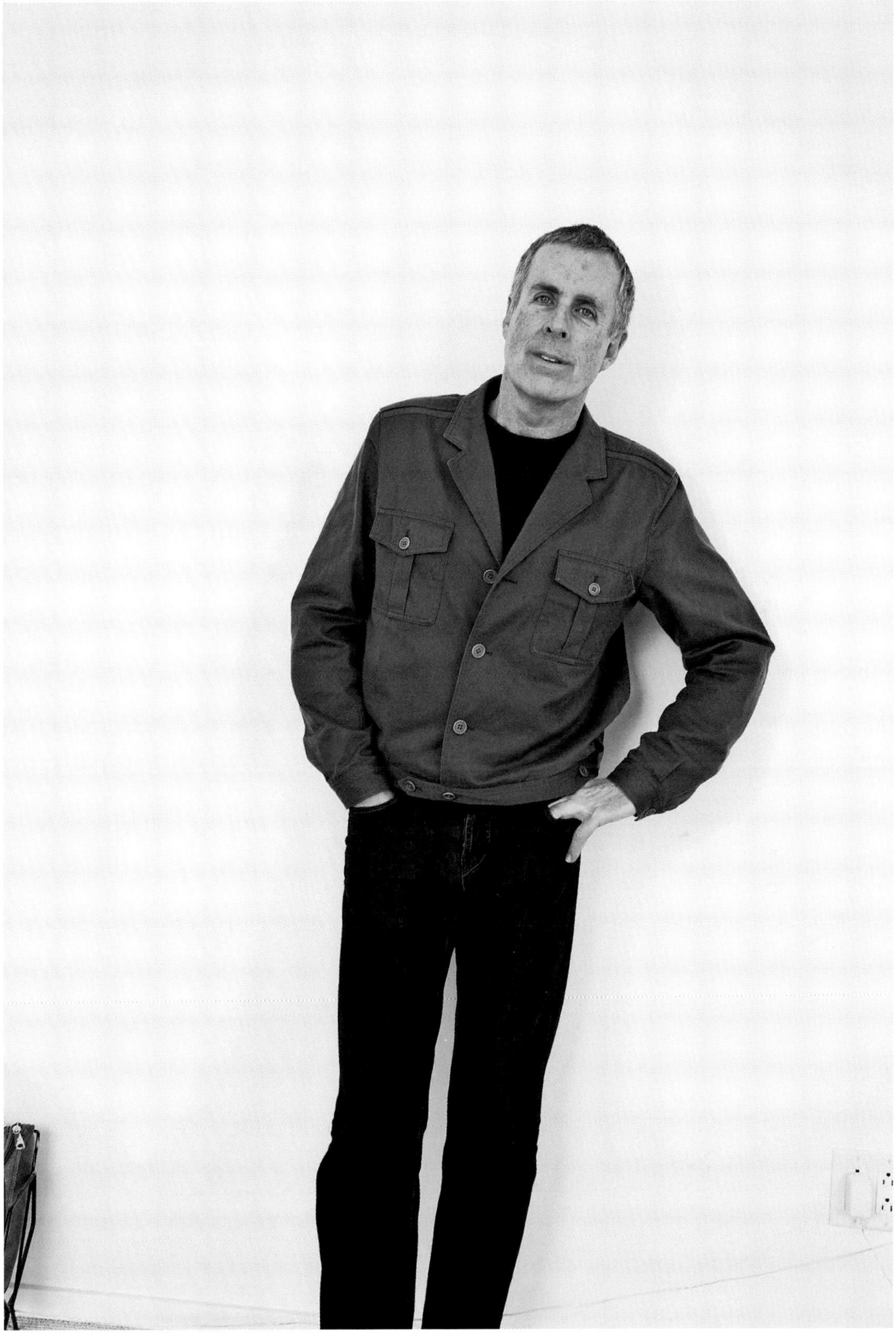

Jaspreet Singh in his apartment on rue Bernard, Outremont, 2001

Jaspreet and a friend visiting from the U.S. received me with what initially felt like a degree of suspicion. Somehow, we quickly got into a discussion about Jaspreet's PhD in chemical engineering, Kashmiri independence, U.S. foreign policy in India, and gay Asians in Canada. What I had felt as suspicion evaporated when we found agreement on a few political points, or perhaps just when we found that we could talk. At that point, we crawled through a bedroom window onto a mossy gravel roof where bricks, tar, and dangling wires set the visual motifs. Back inside, Jaspreet, with an obvious sense of theatrical pleasure, excitedly changed clothes, locations, and postures as ideas occurred to him. It was, in fact, impossible to contain him.

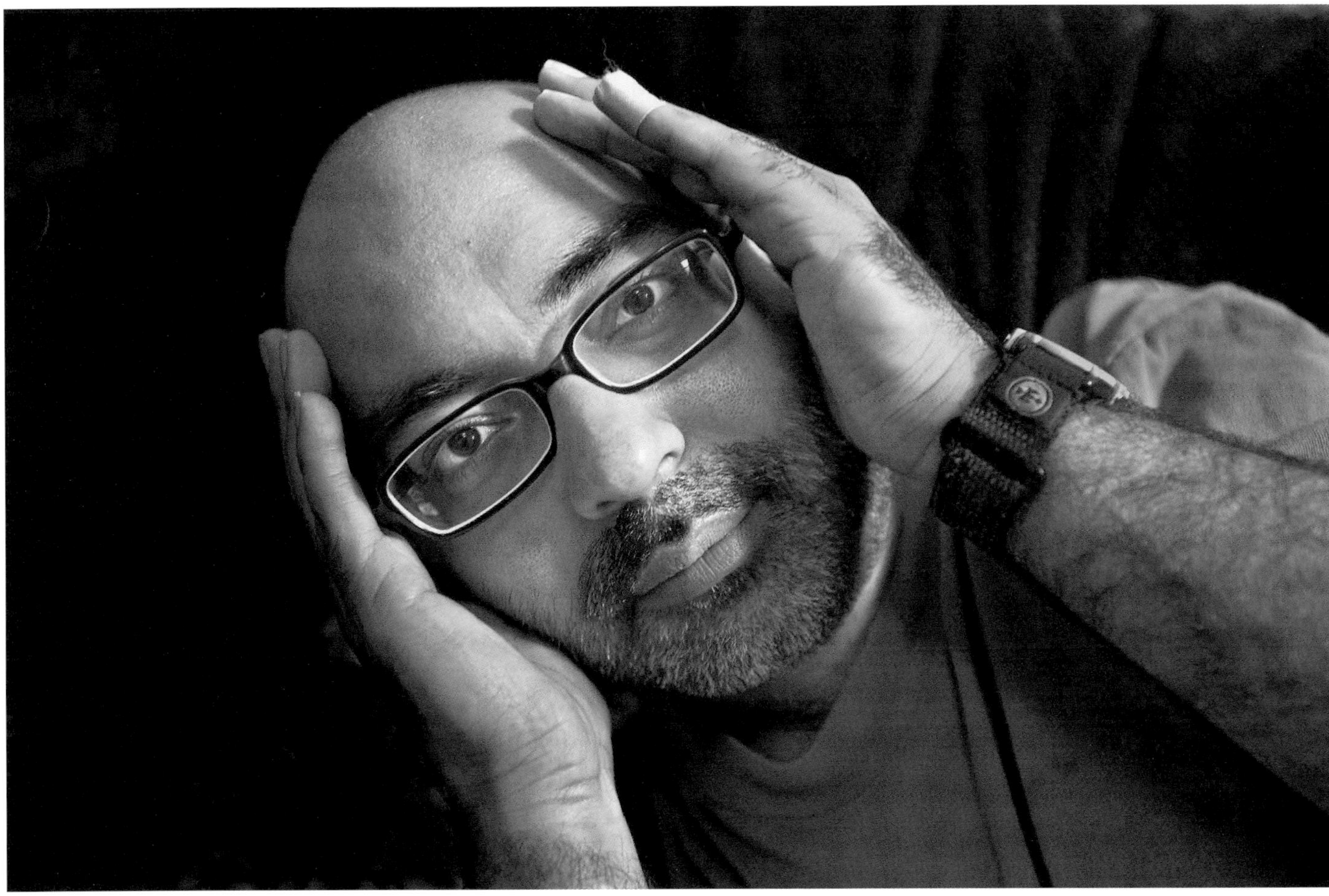

Carolyn Marie Souaid in the courtyard of a pub on Bishop Street in Montreal, November 2003

MY FIRST SHOOT WITH Carolyn Marie Souaid was at her home in a town on the south shore of the St. Lawrence River a few years before this photograph was made. Then, after touring her house, we settled in the kitchen, where Carolyn pointed out the unusual stillness in the room. The kitchen, as it turned out, faced a graveyard, which made her a little uneasy. In the years following, Carolyn's family situation changed, as did the way she thought of home. That's how we wound up in the deserted courtyard of an Irish pub, where she obligingly sat for me on a plastic chair facing a small table with a couple of centimetres of snow on it. Her expression as I took pictures occupied a space between distressed and amused. It was only after she stood up that I saw I had asked my accommodating subject to sit in a pool of slushy snow, and she had not only agreed, but stayed there. Afterwards, Caroline said she had enjoyed both experiences in front of the camera and would consider doing it again with one proviso—she would not sit in any more snow.

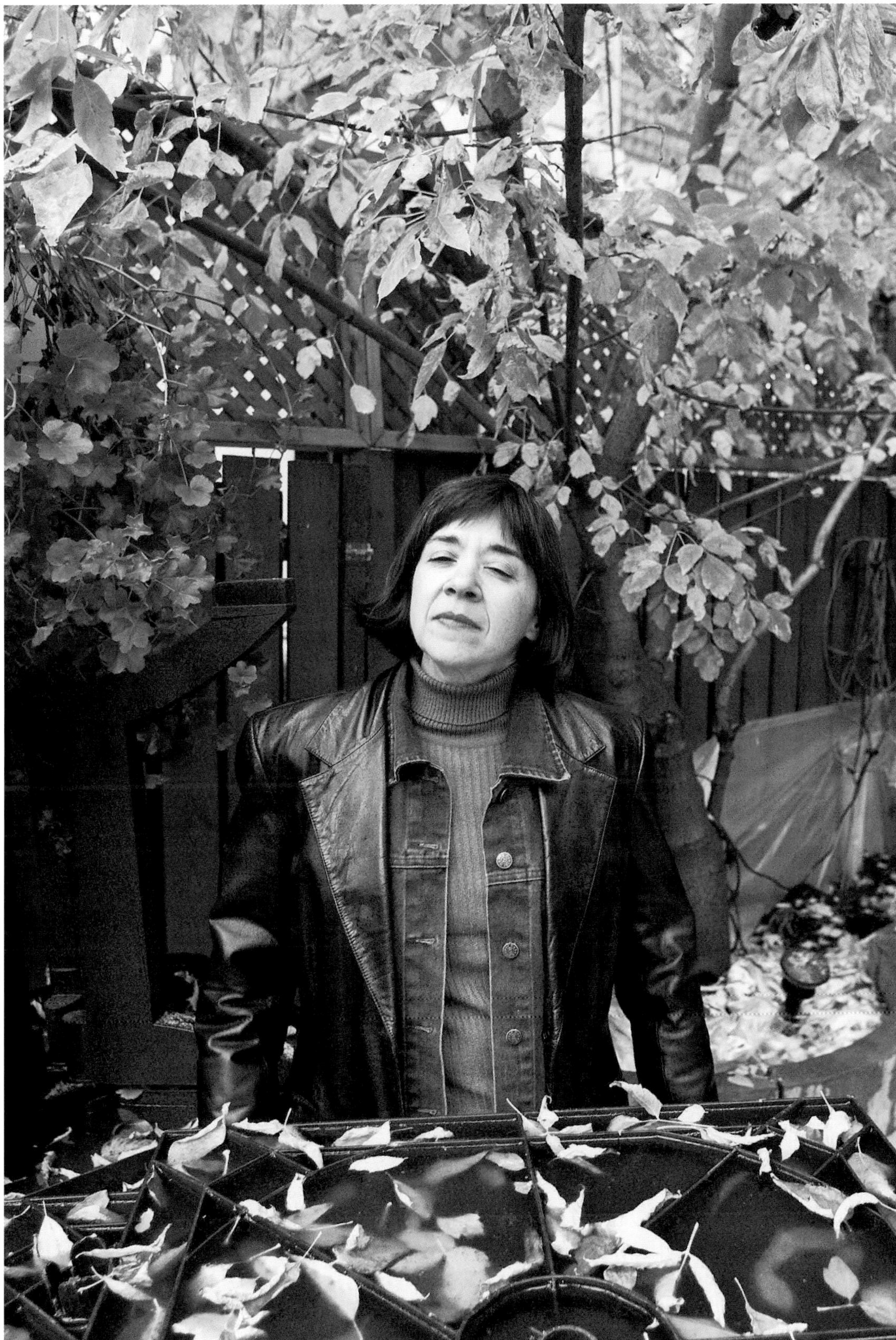

William Weintraub in his Wood Avenue home in Westmount, September 2005

THE LIGHT WAS VERY STRONG when William Weintraub welcomed me into his home, and when I photographed him near a window, he was partly cast in deep shadow. The shapes were handsome enough, but an image with that much darkness in it would have seemed to be saying something about William's long life, which was not what I wanted. His study displayed many signs of a long and successful career, but, except as an illustration of that life, it was visually dull. That is, except for a pinned-up selection of "dirty" postcards—many of them well preserved antiques—from several countries. I encouraged William to mount them on acid-free board but he chuckled at my concern with preserving the past. He was more interested in telling me about the history of vaudeville, striptease, and the remarkable life of Gypsy Rose Lee, for whom he had tremendous admiration. All this as he sat beside a bookcase with titles on comedy writing, nutrition, hippies, bohemians, and a score of other subjects that have occupied the popular imagination for the last 70 or so years. The home of a writer who has lived a long and full life can speak so insistently of the past that it's difficult to find an image that speaks of him in the present.

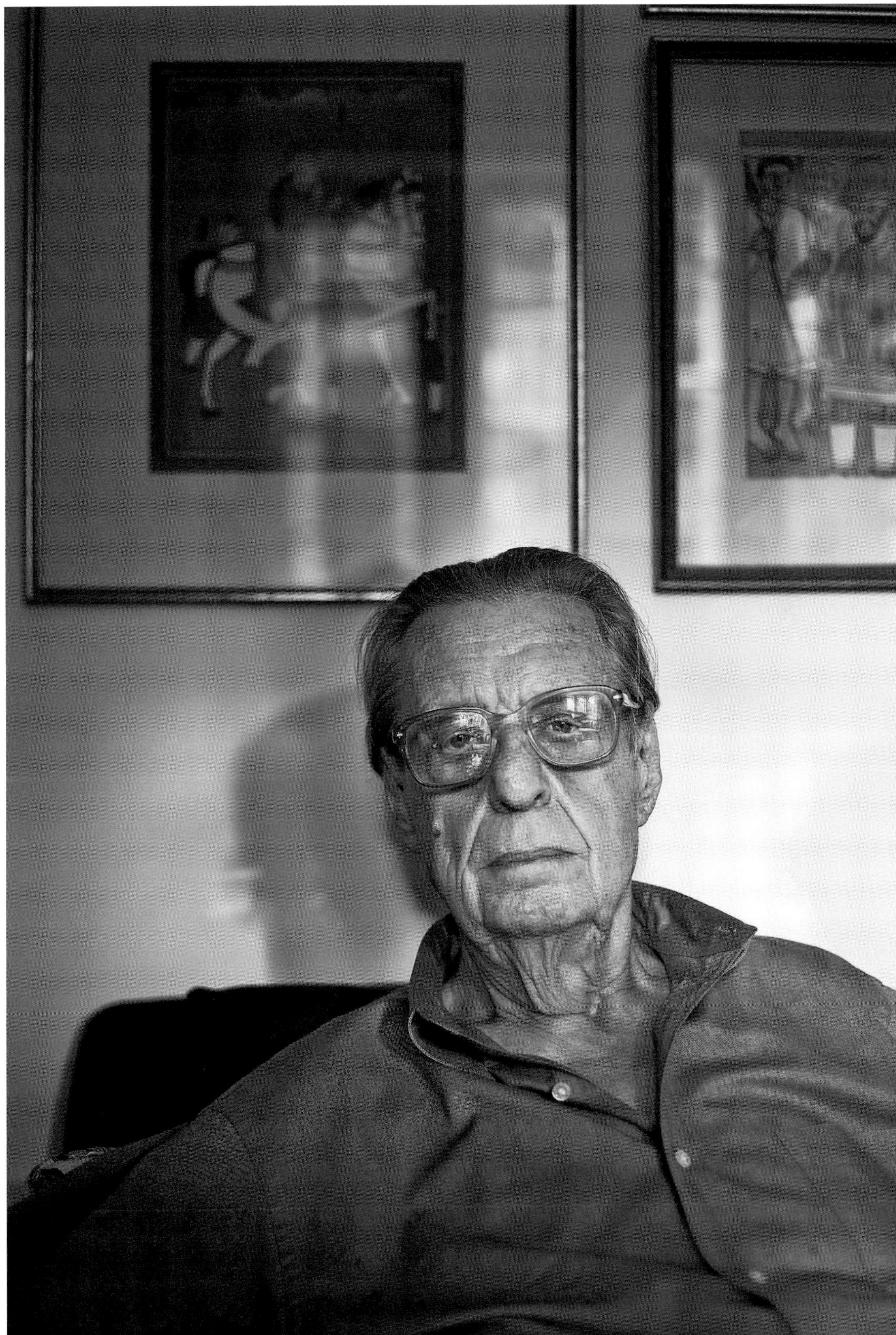

KIT BRENNAN IN HER SUBURBAN HOME ON 53RD AVENUE IN LACHINE, MAY 2000

KIT BRENNAN, unlike most of the writers I photographed, lived in a West Island suburb within walking distance of a commuter train station. We toured her immaculately kept back yard and garden and Kit happily sat amidst some shrubs in a rock garden and in a hammock while I took photographs. Early on in this project of photographing writers, I had noticed that actors and playwrights have an unusual awareness of their own bodies and faces, and of the space around them. In fact, it sometimes seems that their portraits are given rather than made. After we moved inside the house, Kit sat on this steamer trunk from her partner's family. It had begun travelling the world in 1921 but now housed her collection of hats.

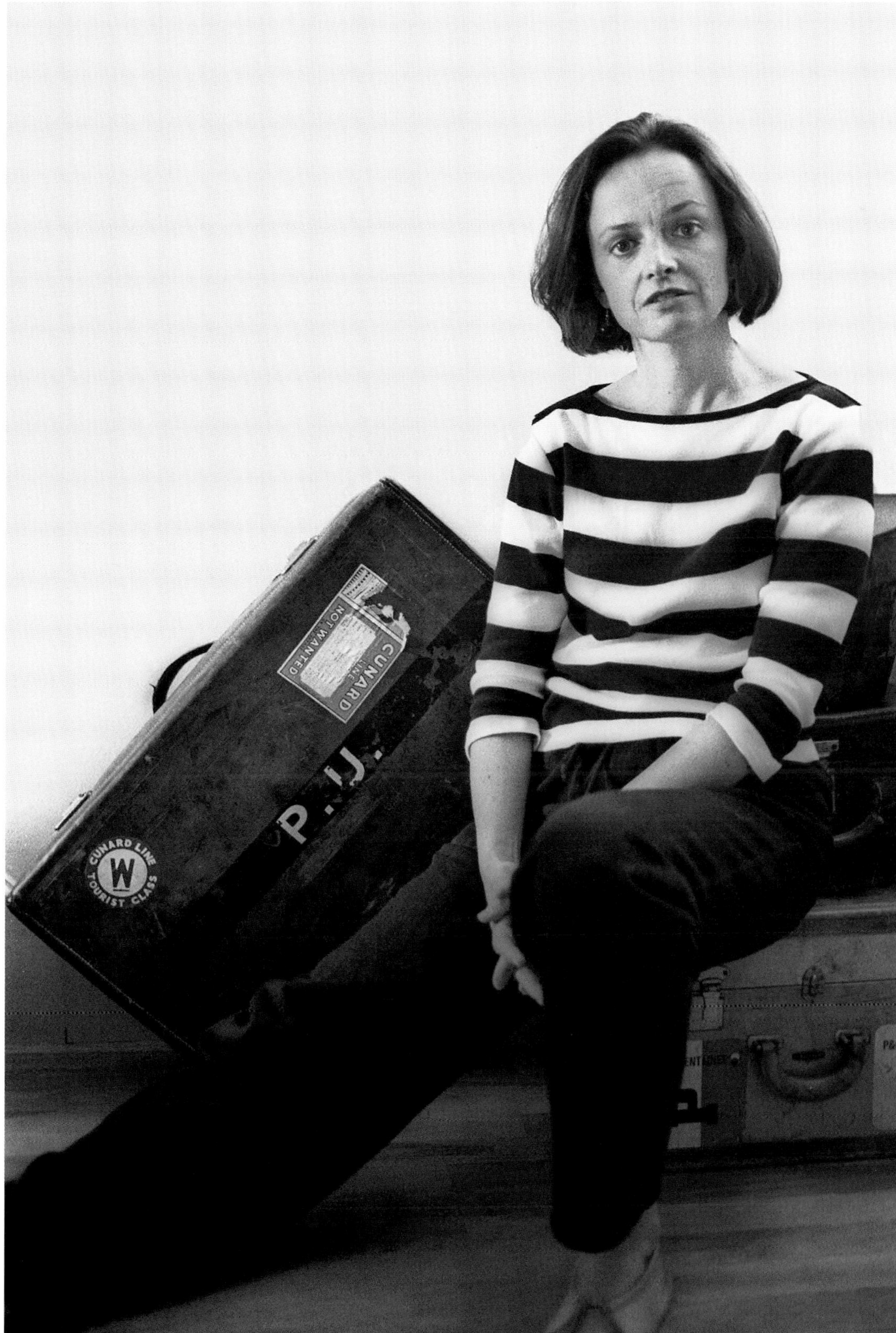
CUNARD
NOT WANTED
P.J.
CUNARD LINE
W
TOURIST CLASS

Raymond Filip in the shell of his home recording studio, Pincourt, November 2007

RAY GREW UP IN THE ROUGH-AND-TUMBLE suburb of Verdun as a member of a tiny Lithuanian community and seemed to cherish his association with place. It was surprising, then, to see the large suburban house he had just bought, the plushy furnishings, and the rooms filled with flowers. The presence of the flowers was soon explained by his wife, an assertive and friendly Filipina who was starting an on-line florist business. She and her sister sat at a long dining room table working on accounts and assembling gift baskets. Ray's mother, who appeared to speak only Lithuanian, kept a close eye on us, gesturing peremptorily when she wanted Ray to do something for her. Ray said that she had recently fallen from her balcony and almost died, but she betrayed no hint of weakness or frailty. We spent most of our time together in Ray's upstairs office looking at his collection of guitars. He is an accomplished musician and was putting together a CD, and asked to be photographed with the vertically held neck of a guitar dividing his face, which is asymmetrical—a quality he badly wanted to emphasize. When we were almost done, he showed me a Penguin anthology of Canadian poetry, carrying it with both hands underneath the book, making me think of the way I had seen someone handle a Gutenberg bible. A few weeks afterward, when Ray wrote me asking about the photograph for the CD, he signed his message, "The Last of the Iconoclasts."

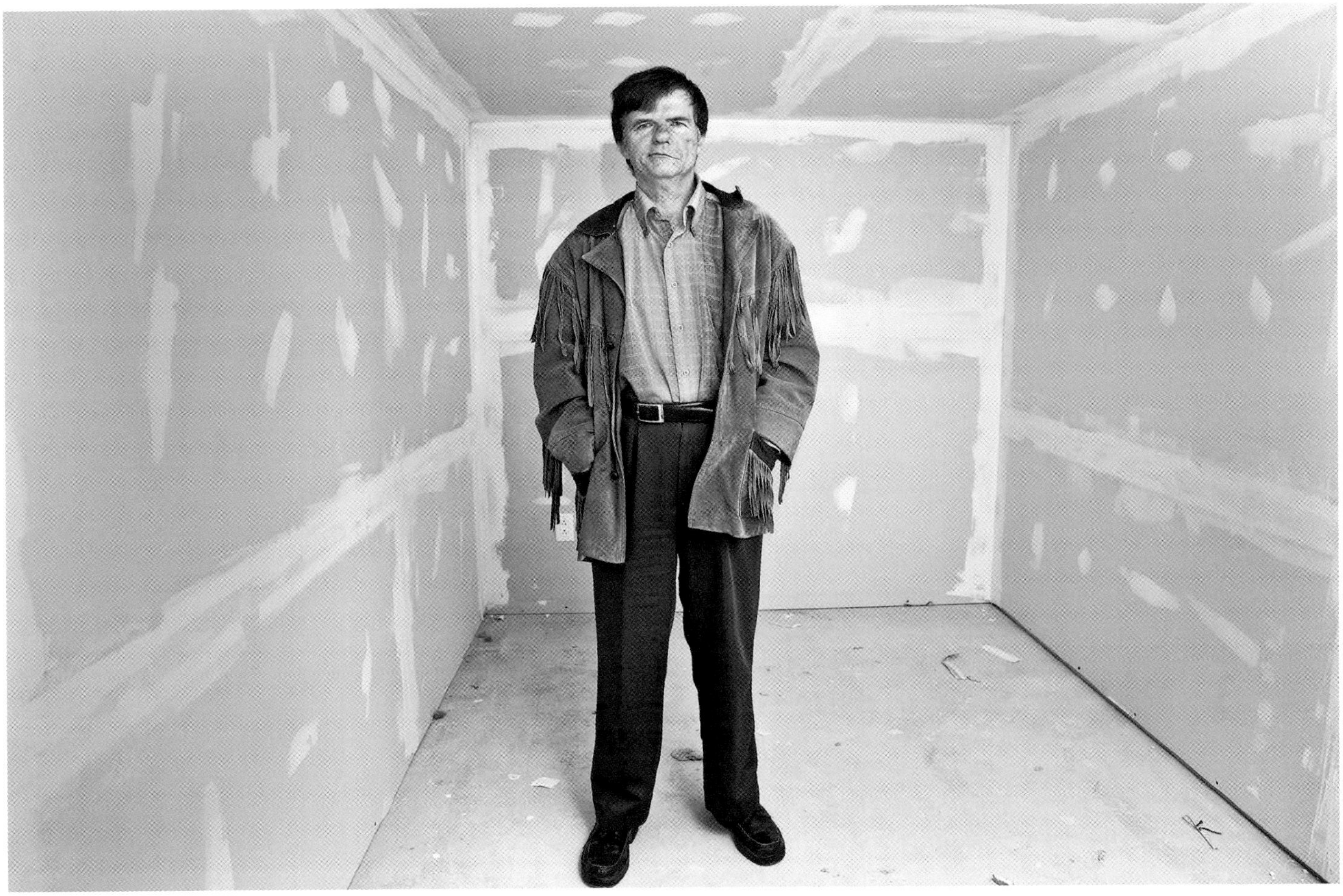

Oana Avasilichioaei in her workroom
on rue St-Urbain, Plateau Mont-Royal, February 2008

Oana's quicksilver expressions reminded me of the illustrations in a 1940s modelling manual that I once rescued from someone's trash bin. In this book, dozens of tiny photographs showed would-be models how to display a variety of emotions. In Oana's case, a down-turned mouth or slightly lowered eyelids signalled dubiousness. Hands folded in her lap and a neutral expression, mild discomfort. A stretched smile with her head tilted back, utter disbelief. After we'd been shooting for an hour, she finally said, with a hint of challenge, "Alright. Why me? Why my picture?" I mentioned her translations from French, her use of fairy tales, her Romanian background, her sense of style, and the utter mystery of her last name's pronunciation, and left it to her to assemble my jumbled response into an answer. Then she relaxed. After the session, she darted back into her workroom and took a bottle of slivovitz from a cabinet, poured us two small glasses, and stood for a moment in front of them. When we raised the glasses, she taught me a Romanian toast: *"Noroc!"*

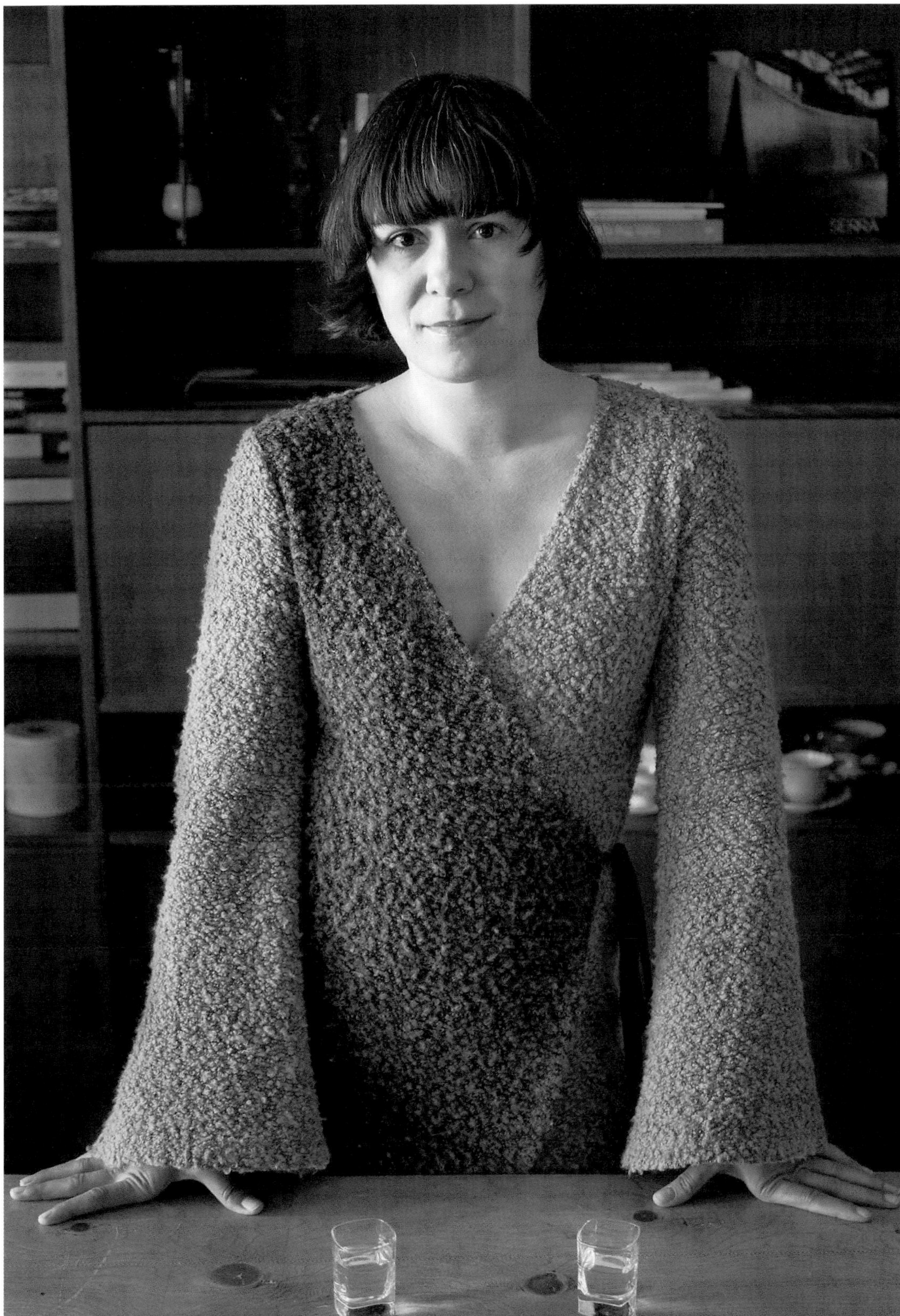

Andrew Steinmetz behind his apartment on rue Waverly, Plateau Mont-Royal, September 2001

WHEN I FIRST MET ANDREW, he was a ward clerk at a Montreal hospital, and had just written a book about that experience. Hippocrates wasn't the resident muse in his home, though. In his bright front room, above a reading stand tucked away in a corner, he had hung a photograph of his great aunt Eva Steinmetz, who is shown playing an accordion in Vienna in the 30s. Eva appeared in a touring version of *The Threepenny Opera*, knew Brecht and Weil, and studied acting with Max Ophuls. Andrew had known his aunt well, owned many photographs of her, and her presence in his imagination gave him a sense of possibility that nourished his notion of himself as a writer. That sense of identity also encouraged him to leave Montreal because, he told me years after our shoot, he had felt a certain "urban provincialism" there and everyone living on the Plateau "reflected everyone else." At the end of our conversation he asked, with hopeful urgency, if our 2001 session in his old home had produced any photographs with Eva's picture in the background, and, if so, could he have a copy?

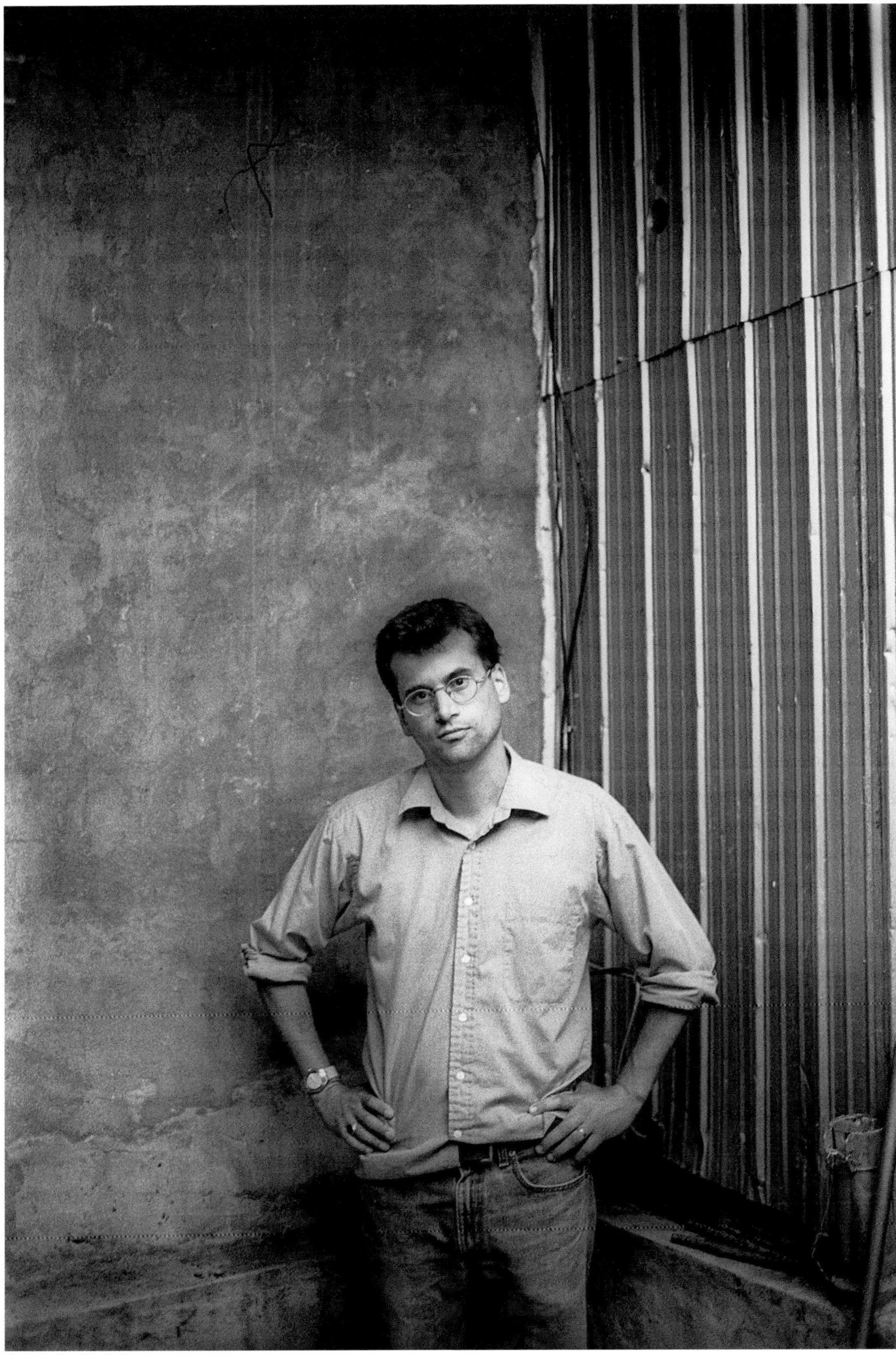

Jeffrey Moore at the baseball diamond in Parc Jeanne-Mance, September 2004

Jeff had a home in the Laurentian Mountains and suggested that the natural attractions of the place would provide a good setting for a photograph. However, it was hard for me to imagine him at ease in nature. I had already photographed him in his dark *pied à terre* not far from Parc Jeanne-Mance, and in the alleyways of Mile End and the Plateau. In those locations, he had a loose-limbed slouch that suggested he wanted to be seen that way. It wasn't until I saw him playing baseball in Parc Jeanne-Mance that the setting and the character seemed to match up. He complained about sore joints, but stood at the plate in tense readiness. His swing seemed to begin late but it was very fast and hard, and connected solidly with almost every pitch. It was in that intense concentration and channelled aggression that I could see the barbed humour of his prose.

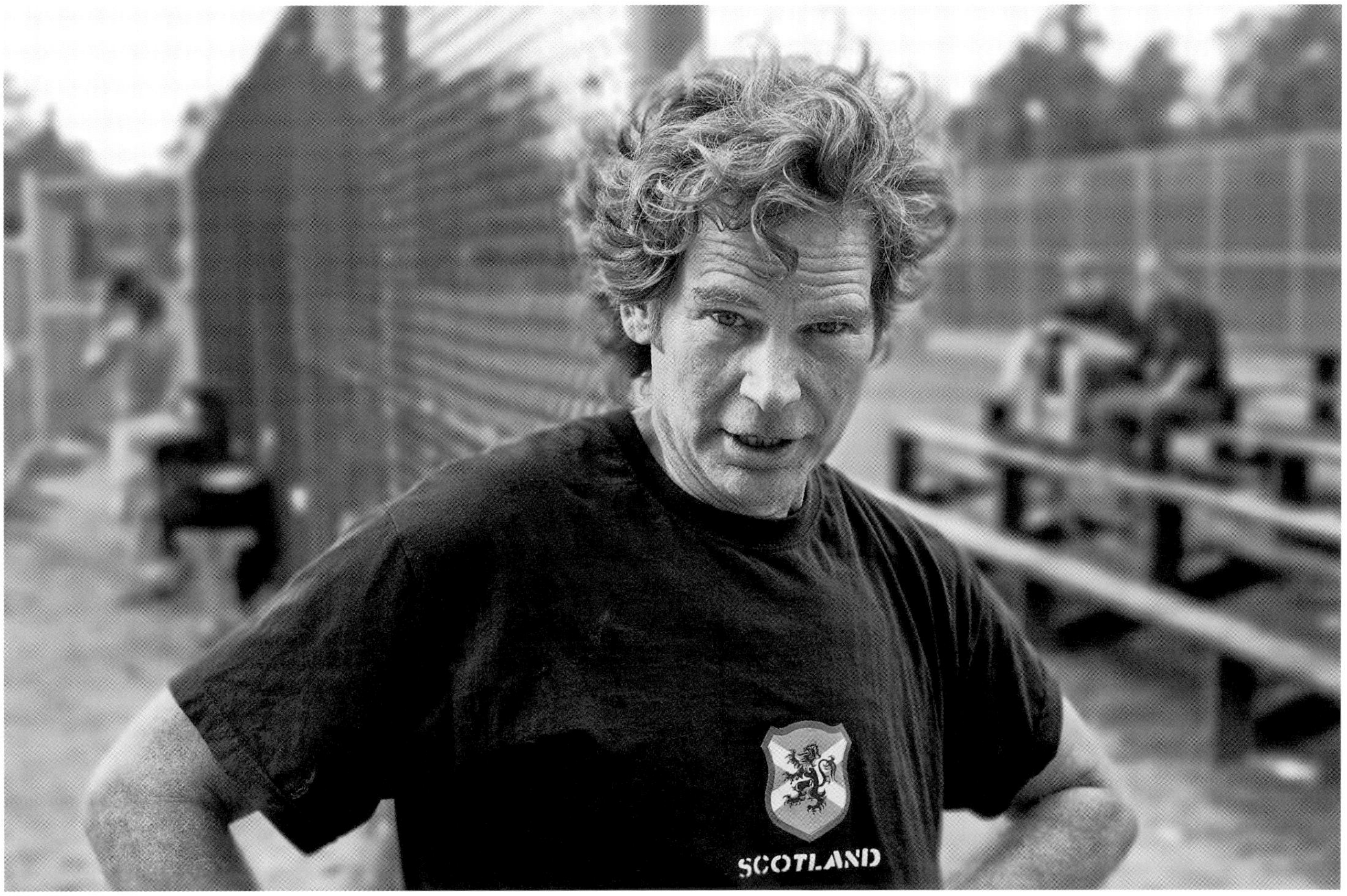
SCOTLAND

ELAINE KALMAN NAVES IN HER KITCHEN, O'BRYAN STREET, NOTRE-DAME-DE-GRÂCE, NOVEMBER 2007

EARLY IN THIS PROJECT, I invented a hypothetical "impossible subject" and amused real subjects by talking about her. The impossible subject was a mature woman, one with a stable relationship and a lovely home. She would meet me at the door wearing a simple black outfit and a string of pearls. Why would she be an impossible subject? Because the rough corners of her life had all been rounded off by ordinary prosperity, and she would insist on being photographed with her chin resting on her hand or her fingertips touching her temple. When Elaine, whom I had not met before, came to the door of her comfortable house in a black outfit and pearls, I was startled to see the hypothetical become real. However, when she told me about her excellent painter and the work being done in her kitchen, I saw some taped-up rolls of protective plastic that would serve us well. To my surprise, Elaine enthusiastically helped me to remove the tape and lower the plastic curtain, making a little theatre of her own domesticity. Later, when I told Elaine about having seen her as the impossible subject, she gently chided me with the reminder that her life was not all "rounded corners" and I put the impossible subject to rest.

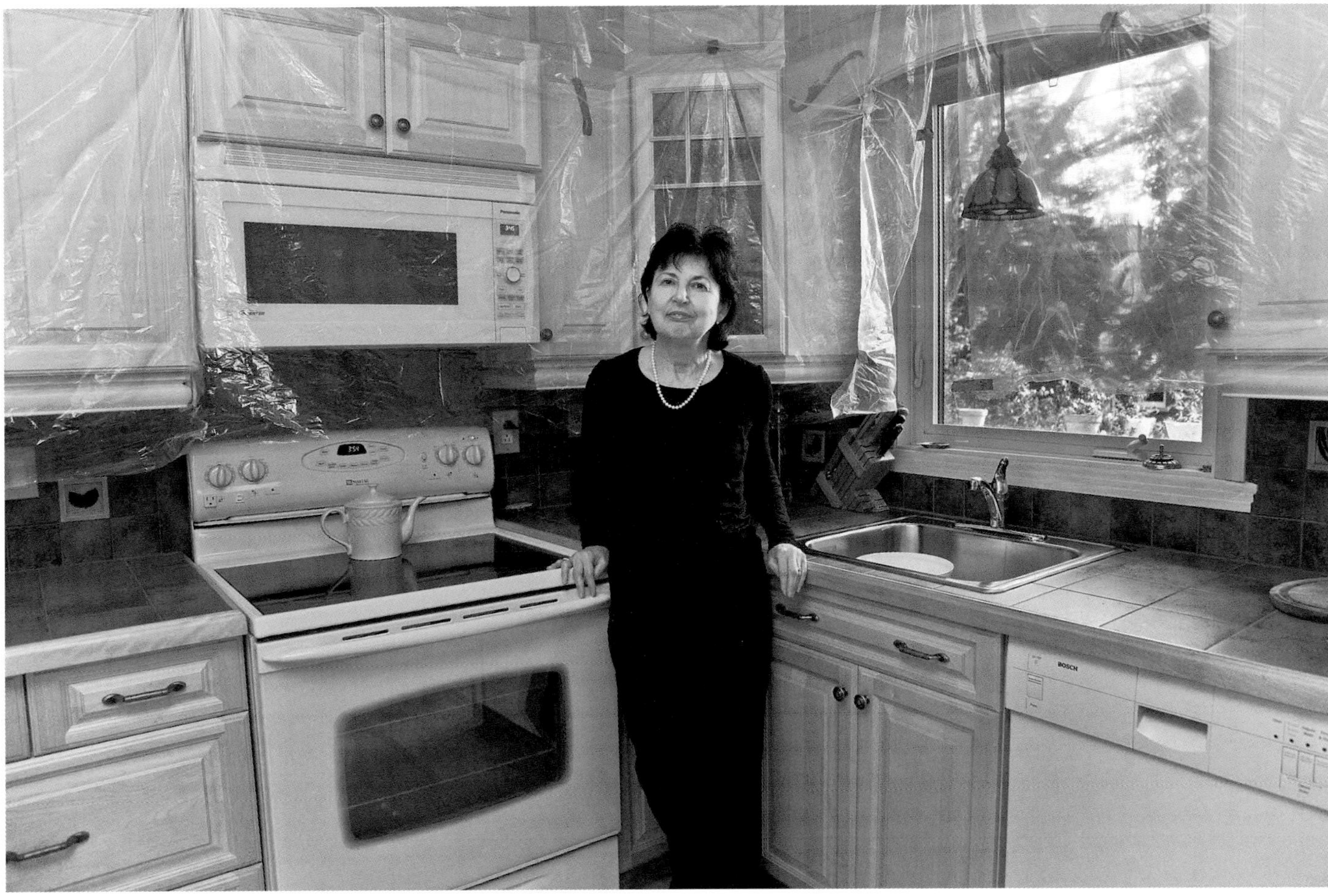

Kent Stetson in his apartment

on Av. Christophe-Colombe in La Petite-Patrie, December 2007

Kent had recently returned from Paris, where, he told me with a mixture of pleasure and consternation, his translator had made fun of his slippers, which he proudly showed off. Finally, the translator decided that "it must be an English thing." Kent was in high spirits because of the continental production of his plays and because he was about to receive the Order of Canada. He had offered—not jokingly, I had hoped—to stand in a snow bank wearing his tuxedo and his Order of Canada medal. Sadly, it wasn't to be presented for another couple of months, so he was safe. We discussed novel-writing, which he was a little concerned about because, with his growing success, his publisher wanted him to move into the fiction market. Somehow, we got onto the topic of a woman I had known, in her 80s, who had survived tuberculosis and great poverty in the early years of the last century, became a political radical, and travelled to Mexico with three other young women to ally themselves with the leftist and anarchist elements in Mexico after the revolution. Kent became very quiet while I told the story, then looked at me seriously, and asked, "Do you think it would make a play?"

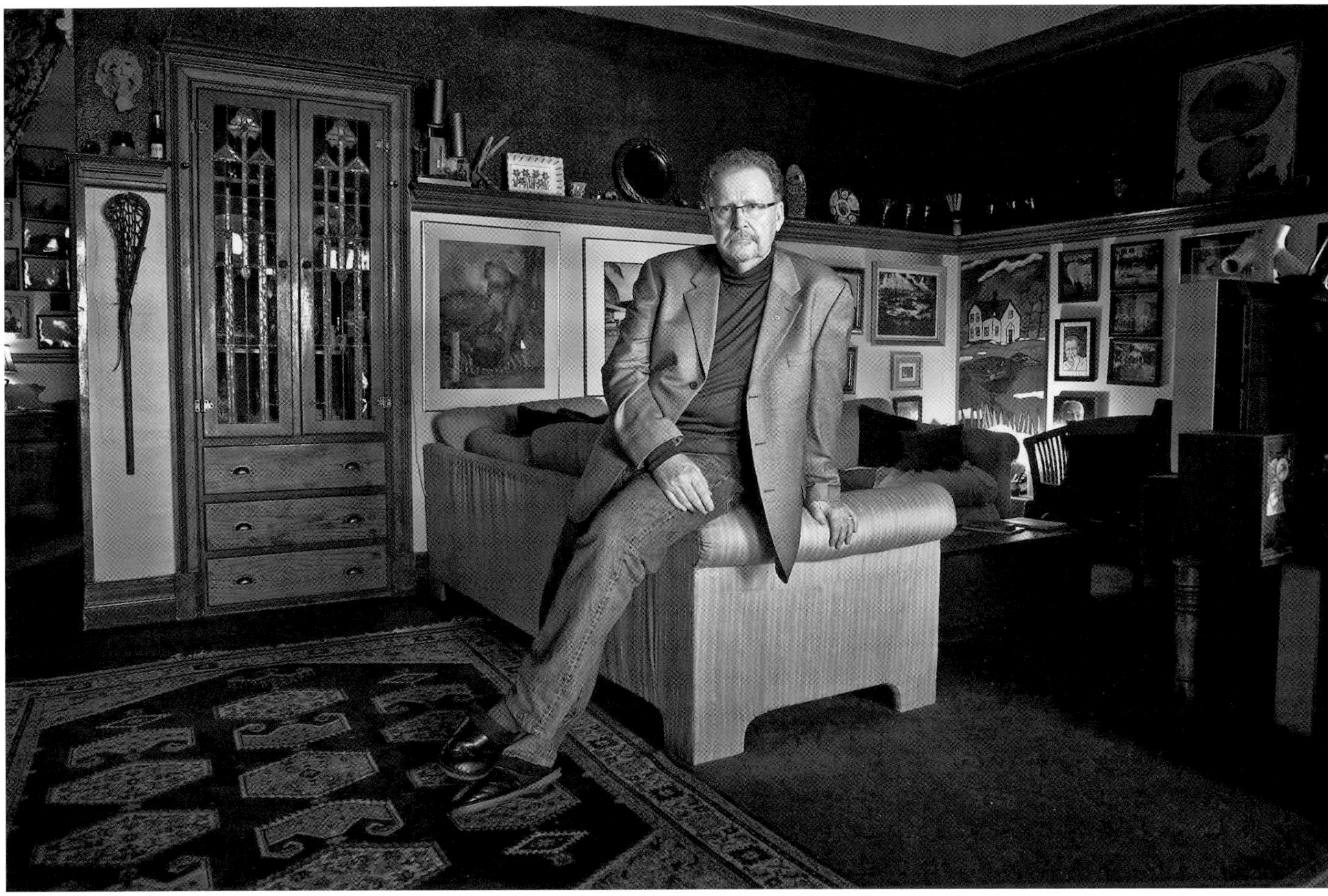

KATE STERNS IN HER KITCHEN,
AV. DE L'ESPLANADE, PLATEAU MONT-ROYAL, AUGUST 2002

KATE HAD RECENTLY RETURNED from long residence in England, by way of the United States, but her speech was still marked by pronunciations that afflict Anglophones who spend years listening to accents from the rest of the Commonwealth. She was not at ease for much of the shoot, and her postures and expressions changed abruptly. My reflexes were usually a half-second too slow to catch them. The room she wrote in held a bed as well as a word processor and when I asked her to rest on the bed, she became distinctly uncomfortable. She was at ease in movement, though, and we ranged from room to room, stopping only long enough for a snapshot with her husband, seated on a couch with ragged upholstery and half a dozen large pillows. When we wandered into the kitchen, she immediately saw my eye catch her playfully labelled cabinets (the worrisome combination "cookies/wine/ham" was just outside the frame on the left) and said, "Oh, no. Not that!"

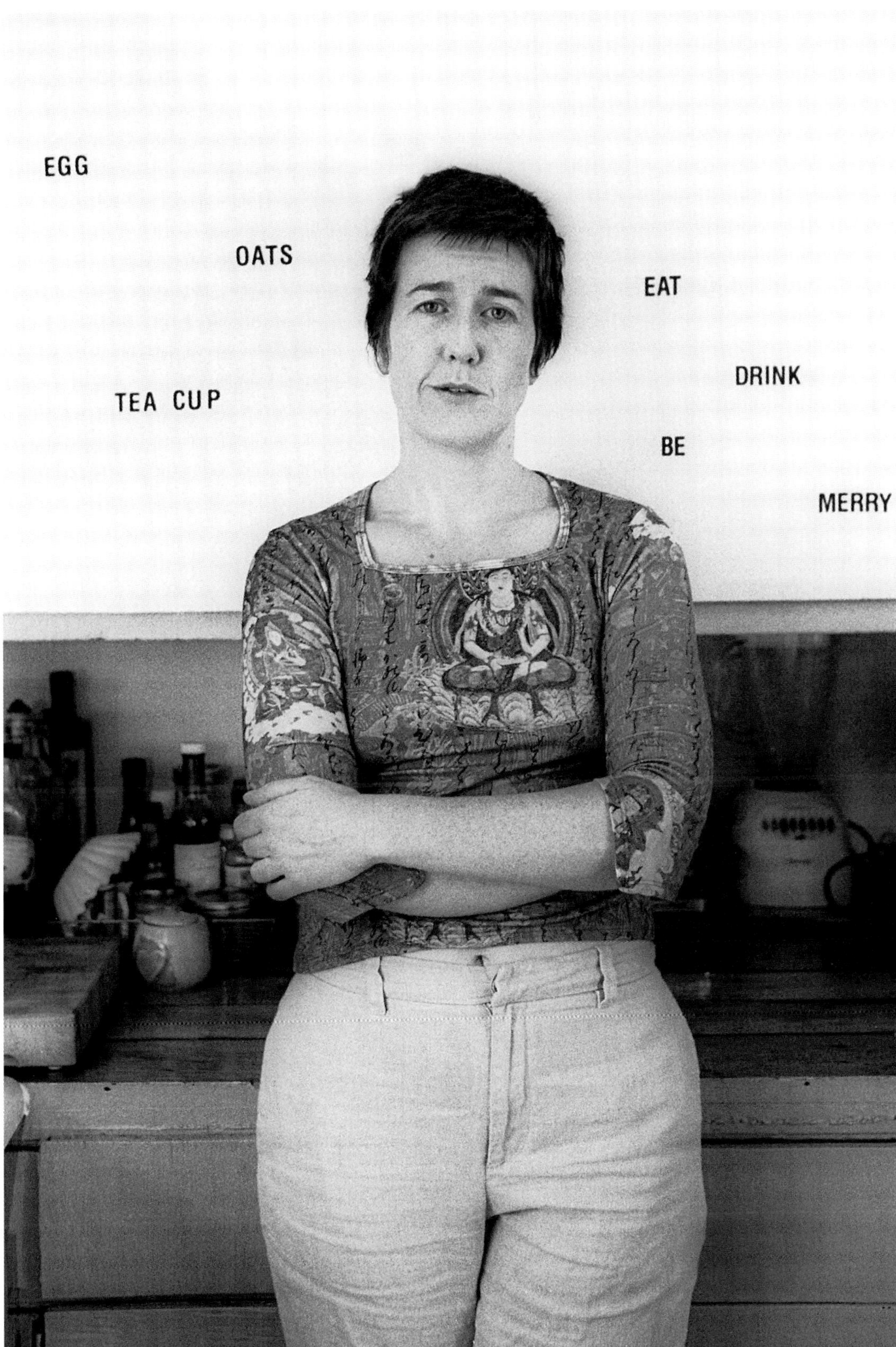
EGG
OATS
EAT
DRINK
TEA CUP
BE
MERRY

ROBERT MAJZELS IN AN ALLEYWAY
NEAR HIS APARTMENT BUILDING, MILE END, SEPTEMBER 1998

ROBERT'S MANNER SHIFTED from impatience to bitterness to humour as the discussion ranged over a broad and unlikely range of topics. Originally from Belgium, he characterized Brussels, dismissively, as "a suburb of Paris." He spoke with discomfort about his youthful difficulties, as a Francophone Jew, fitting into any of the categories Quebec society provided. When he told me about having been a cab driver, his shoulders lifted in sympathy and exasperation at a drunken passenger from the suburb of Verdun who refused to pay the fare. He had left that profession years before, though, travelled, and become a writer whose interests combined politics and literary theory. The last topic we discussed was his time in the Philippines, where he lived with anti-government guerillas. "Some problems," he said, with obvious discomfort, "are only solved with blood."

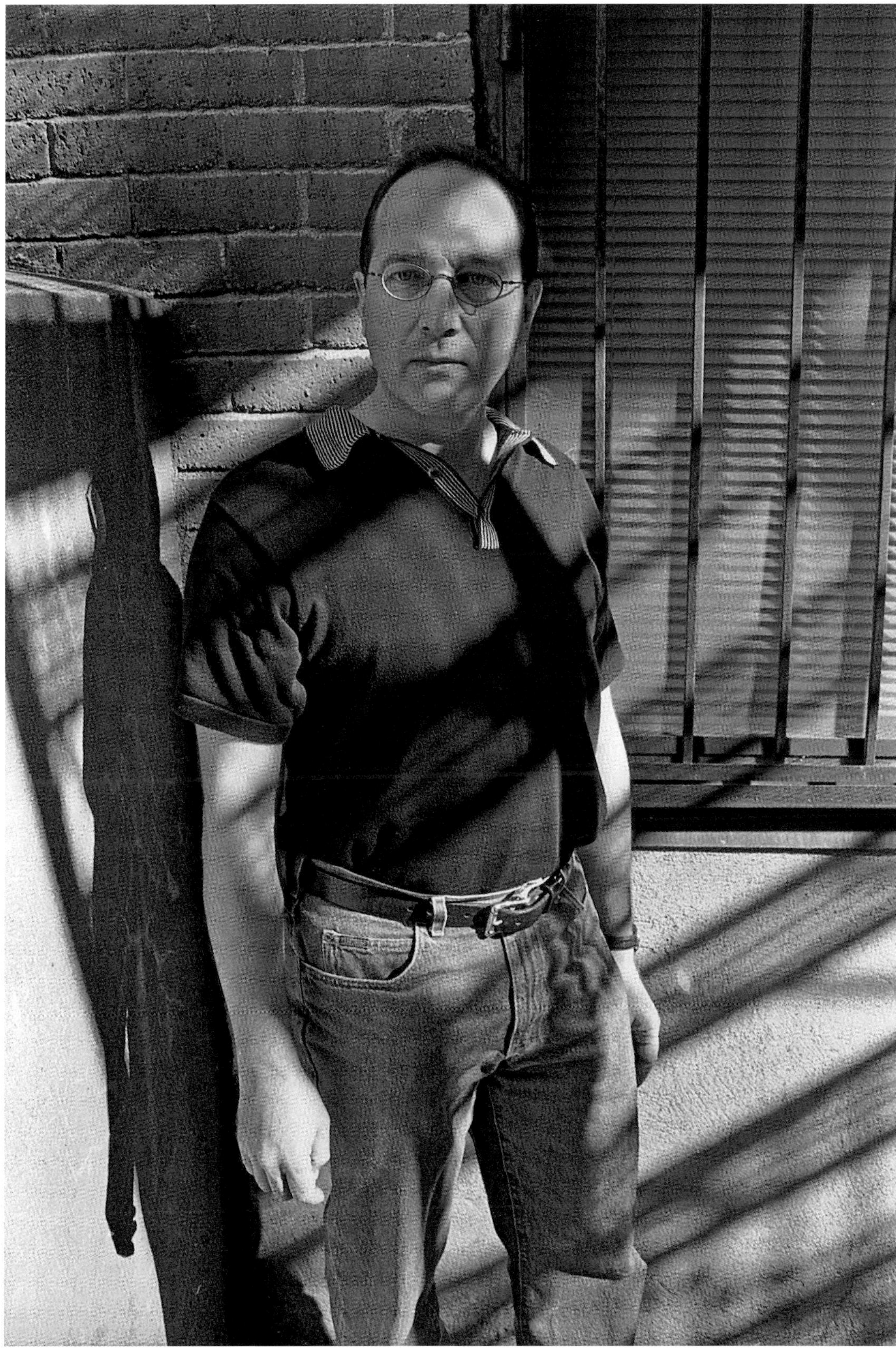

Marianne Ackerman in her kitchen, rue Waverly, Plateau Mont-Royal, November 2007

MARIANNE HAD RECENTLY BEEN IN FRANCE, where she conducted a playwriting workshop in Provence. Her living room was dominated by a towering painting, by her daughter, of an old couple. The woman, in sturdy heels, was painted only from the knees down, as though the rest of her was waiting to be invented. In the basement, among other large paintings, Marianne rummaged for costumes from her theatrical productions and willingly shivered in the front yard, wearing a period dress that put me in mind of Arthurian fantasy while amused passersby watched us. Marianne knew how to be the centre of attention. When I suggested that we clear off her kitchen counter and that she pose on it, she hesitated only for a moment. Later, discussing her next novel, she talked about her move from theatre to fiction. "I'm trying," she said, in tones of frustration that were both real and ironic, "to re-brand myself."

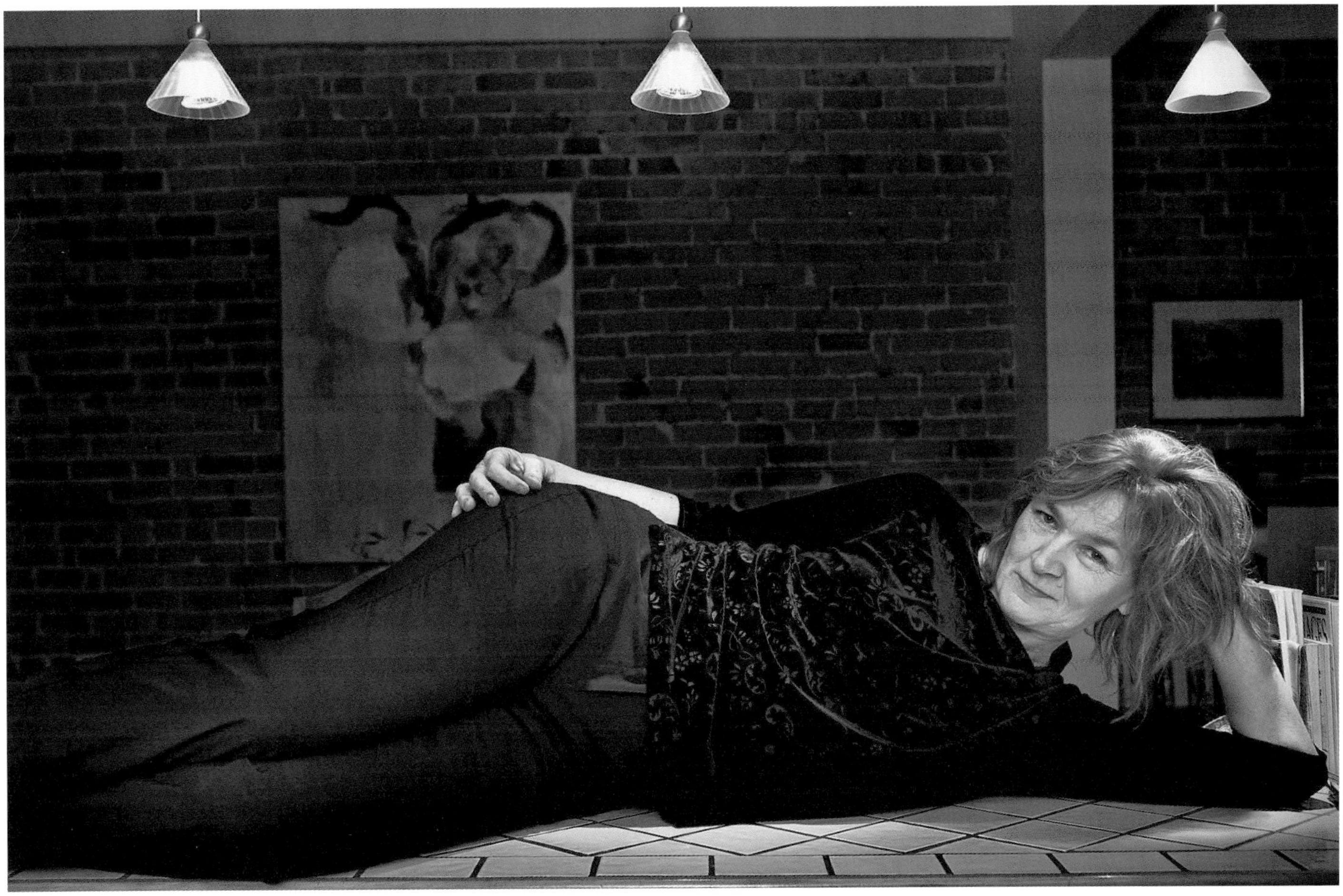

JULIAN SHER IN HIS HOME OFFICE
ON CÔTE ST-ANTOINE, WESTMOUNT, NOVEMBER 2007

WHEN I ARRIVED EXACTLY ON TIME for our shoot, Julian opened the door with an approving smile and said, "You keep journalists' time." He was getting ready for a trip to Afghanistan, reporting for the CBC. This included growing a beard so he would attract less attention. He had reservations about being photographed wearing a beard, but he shouldn't have. His physical solidity, energy, and focus made a much greater impression. When we talked, I tried to draw out his feelings about the potential dangers of his forthcoming project, but he would not let me lead him from the professional to the personal. Mid-way through the shoot, as we walked briskly through his spacious home, he introduced his housekeeper. She put down her dustpan to say hello and I stopped to speak with her for a moment while Julian walked on ahead. I quietly told her that the house looked great. Julian, two rooms away, as alert as an animal, responded, "Thank you!"

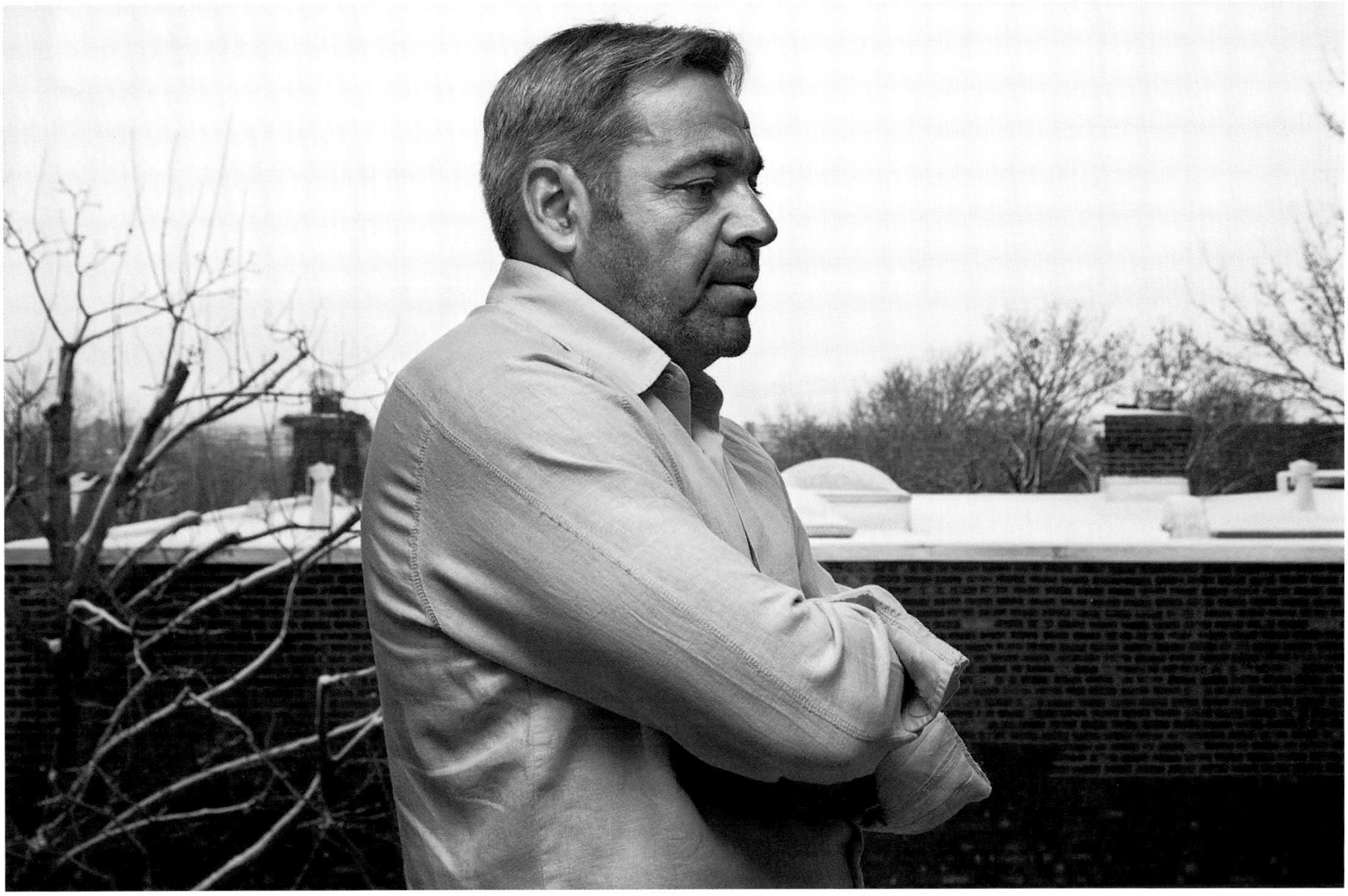

Jon Paul Fiorentino in his apartment on rue St-Urbain, Plateau Mont-Royal, November 2007

JON PAUL WASN'T HAPPY to be photographed in his basement apartment, which was festooned with Christmas lights and drying towels. He was anxious that interior photographs might "deliver the wrong kind of narrative." Later, he pointed out some scars on his lip, concerned about the way they looked, and told me the story behind them. The previous winter, he had stopped a man from beating up a woman on the street, and the man had turned on him. The sidewalk was icy and Jon Paul fell and was hurt but, he said, smiling, "The other guy woke up hurting, too. I whaled on him." As we continued to photograph, it became clear that Jon Paul was a natural model and could create a sense of immediacy and drama from just his posture. He had, it seemed, a gift for making an unfocussed gaze seem filled with meaning.

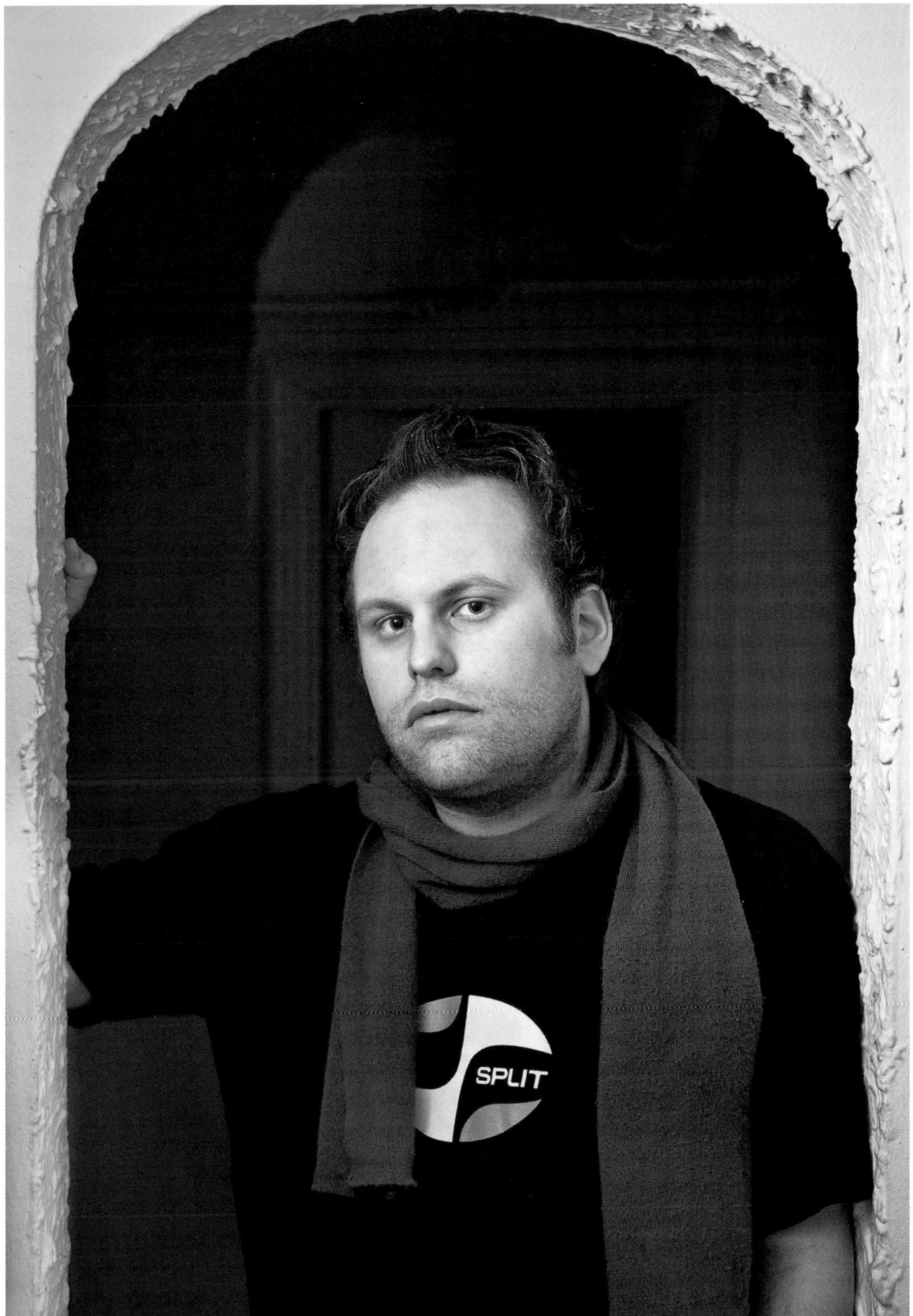
SPLIT

David Solway at the home of his friend Michael Harris, Lower Westmount, September 1999

CONTEMPORARY LITERARY SALONS serve the same function as those of the eighteenth century. They provide status for the host, who must be able to afford them, and a meeting place for writers, who drink their host's fine wine and liquor, and talk. Michael Harris regularly hosted dinners and parties for internationally known writers and for a few locals who were sometimes seen as a reactionary gentleman's club by other writers. Poet, essayist, and *provocateur* David Solway, a friend and frequent guest of Michael's, was entirely at ease knowing this. His direct gaze, untroubled by the camera, signals his awareness that he is comfortable with his public identity and probably aware of the additional *cachet* lent by the sensual art that surrounds him in the photograph. For David, it may have been a moment of feeling like a character in a Hogarth engraving.

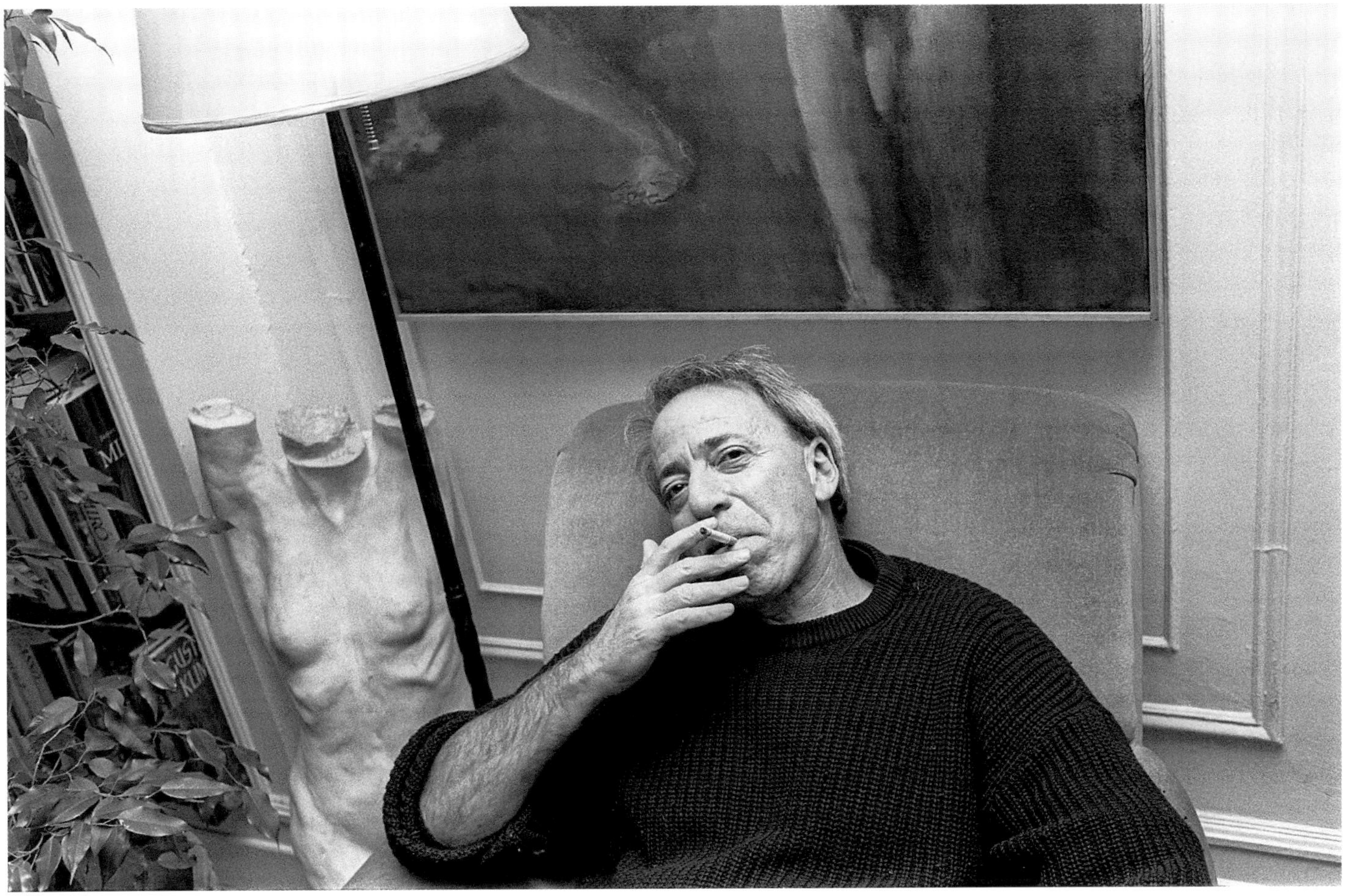

JULIE KEITH AT THE FRONT DOOR
OF HER HOUSE ON ARLINGTON AVENUE IN WESTMOUNT, OCTOBER 1999

JULIE WAS AN ATHLETE as well as a precise and nuanced writer of the disturbances of upper middle class life. That wasn't what we talked about, though. We covered race relations in the U.S., university recruiting, and current politics. When we finished shooting in the house and walked to a nearby café that served people on a sidewalk terrace in the bright but blustery October weather, I was aware of her attractive ranginess and the physical vigour of her movements. Her manner was blithe and ironic as I moved around her taking pictures, and the other patrons at the cafe were openly curious about the tall blonde woman who was being photographed. I was worried at having agreed to shoot in a café because public locations make subjects assume public poses. We returned to her house and said goodbye, but as I stepped out her front door, light filled the entranceway. At that moment, Julie's hands briefly touched as though communicating in a private semaphore. Her direct gaze and physical poise were less ambiguous, though. Everything about her seemed to say *I'm ready*.

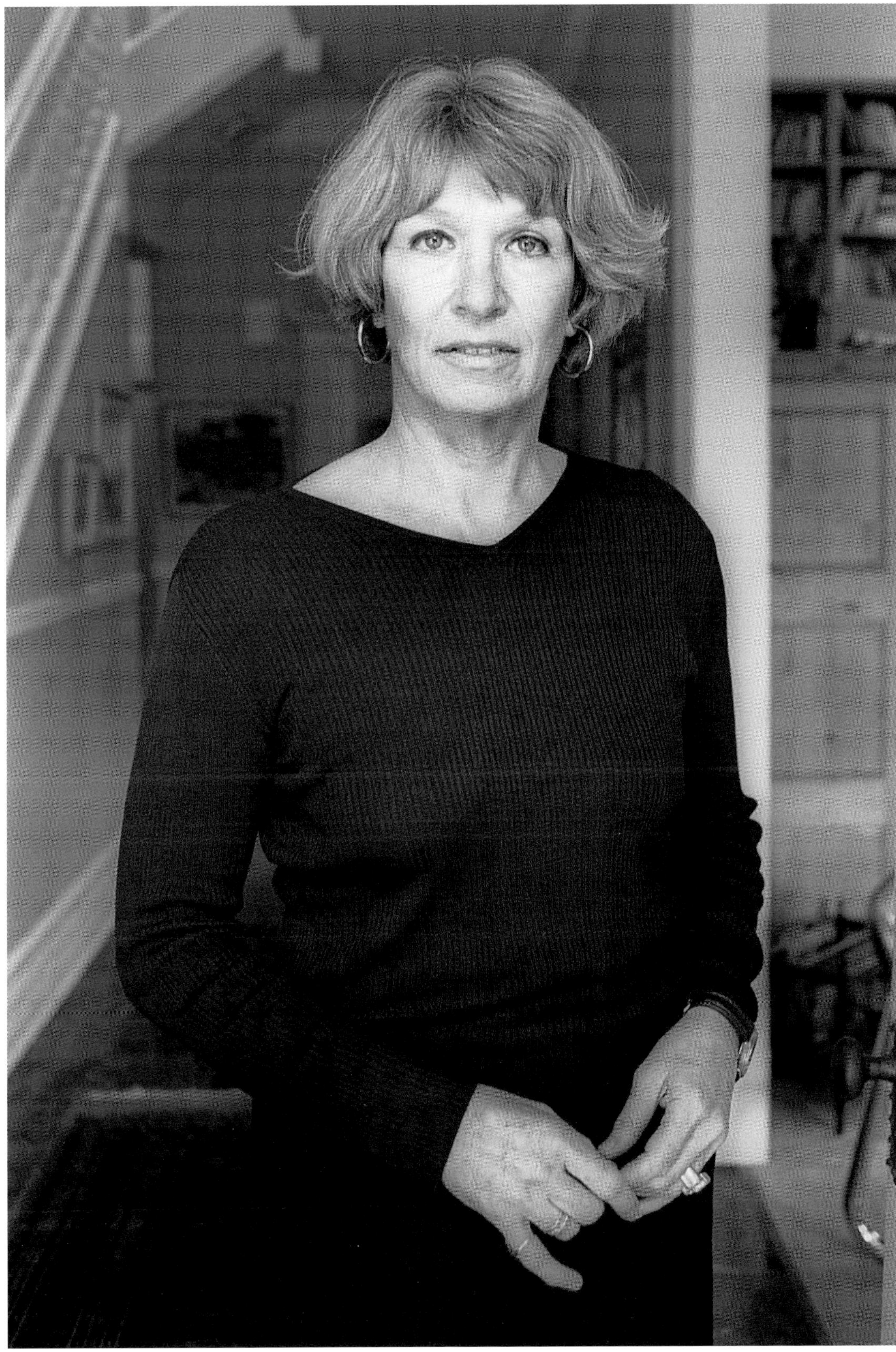

Andy Brown in his building

on rue St-Dominique, Plateau Mont-Royal, December 2007

ANDY'S STRETCH OF RUE ST-DOMINIQUE is a graceless combination of modern, low-rise apartment buildings and nineteenth-century working class residences, some with *porte-cochères* that must have once led to stables or courtyards but now open on back yards. The ceilings of the older buildings are low and droopy, and the maple or birch floors sag under the weight of their age. Andy bought one of these buildings, complete with its long-time tenants, and renovated part of it for a home and part for his small publishing company, Conundrum Press. In his office, he opened an old-fashioned tan suitcase to show me treasures of counterculture publishing and graphic novels. Andy was nothing if not game. Although he was fighting off a cold and generally feeling unwell, he trooped into the back yard to plant himself in four feet of snow for a photograph. There was in his manner a suggestion of willingness to shoulder burdens and to have a life whose financial and professional rewards will always be uncertain.

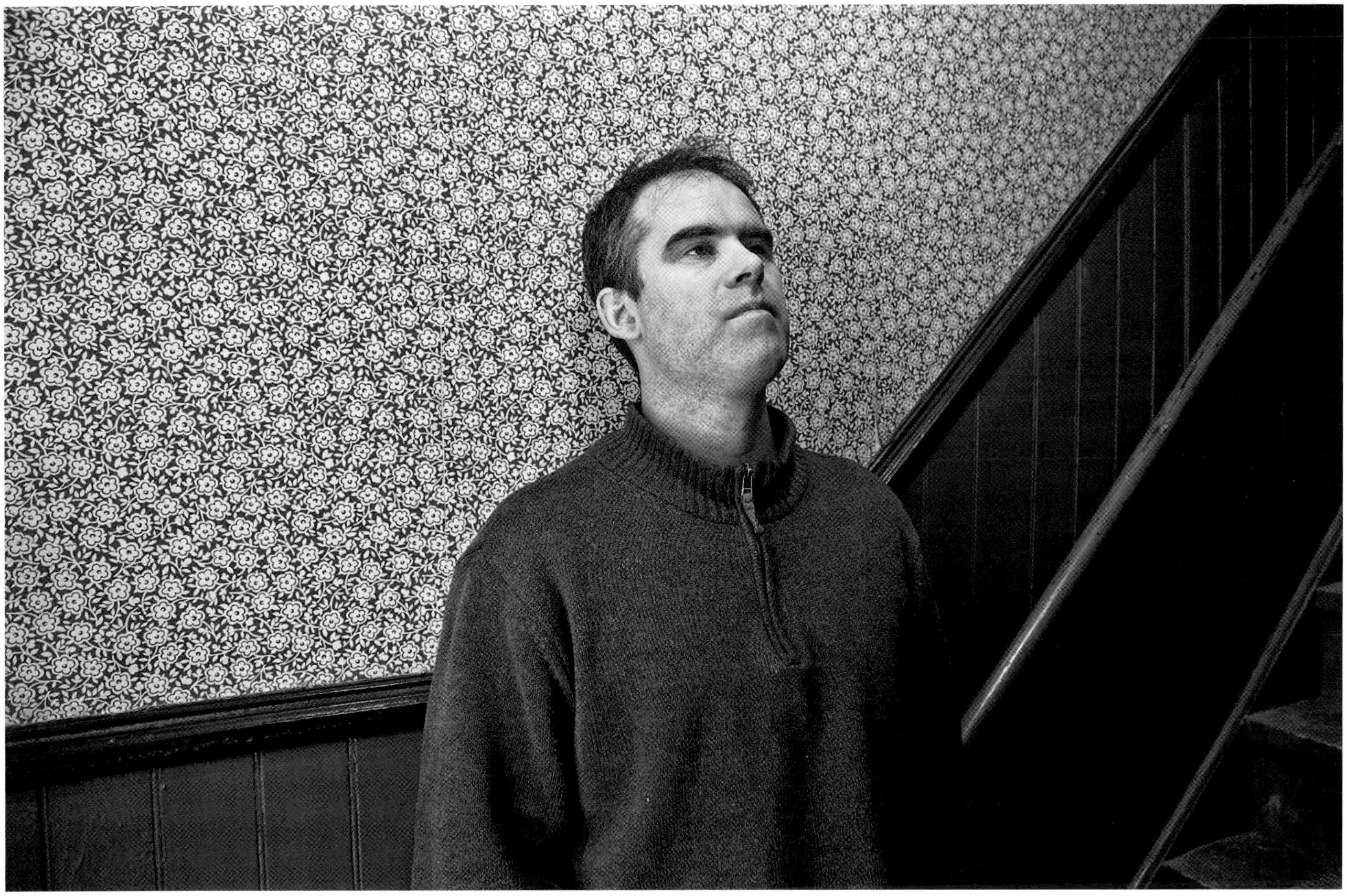

CATHERINE KIDD ON A ROOF

ON BOULEVARD ST-LAURENT, PLATEAU MONT-ROYAL, APRIL 2000

ONE DAY, A WOMAN who at first glance I took to be a bag lady showed up at my door and asked to talk. After a stunned moment, I realized that the woman was Catherine Kidd, but looking as I had never seen her before. She haltingly explained that she was heavily medicated and seriously ill and had been diagnosed with a pituitary disorder. Her heart, she said, was beating as fast as a hummingbird's. She talked about having being shown an X-ray with a suspicious butterfly shape on her pituitary, but she declined surgery because she felt the shape was so beautiful it couldn't do harm. When I next saw Catherine, she appeared to have miraculously cured herself with a dietary regimen and running. She also used an old-fashioned vibrating machine of the sort that was supposed to shake off pounds because she felt that the harmful forces in her brain might be shaken out through the soles of her feet. The next time I saw her, she seemed to be glowing with health, as was her career as a literary performance artist. She held a large iguana on her shoulder and told a story about losing it out the window of her second-storey apartment and, as I recall, the iguana having taken an extended ride on the roof of someone's car before she got it back.

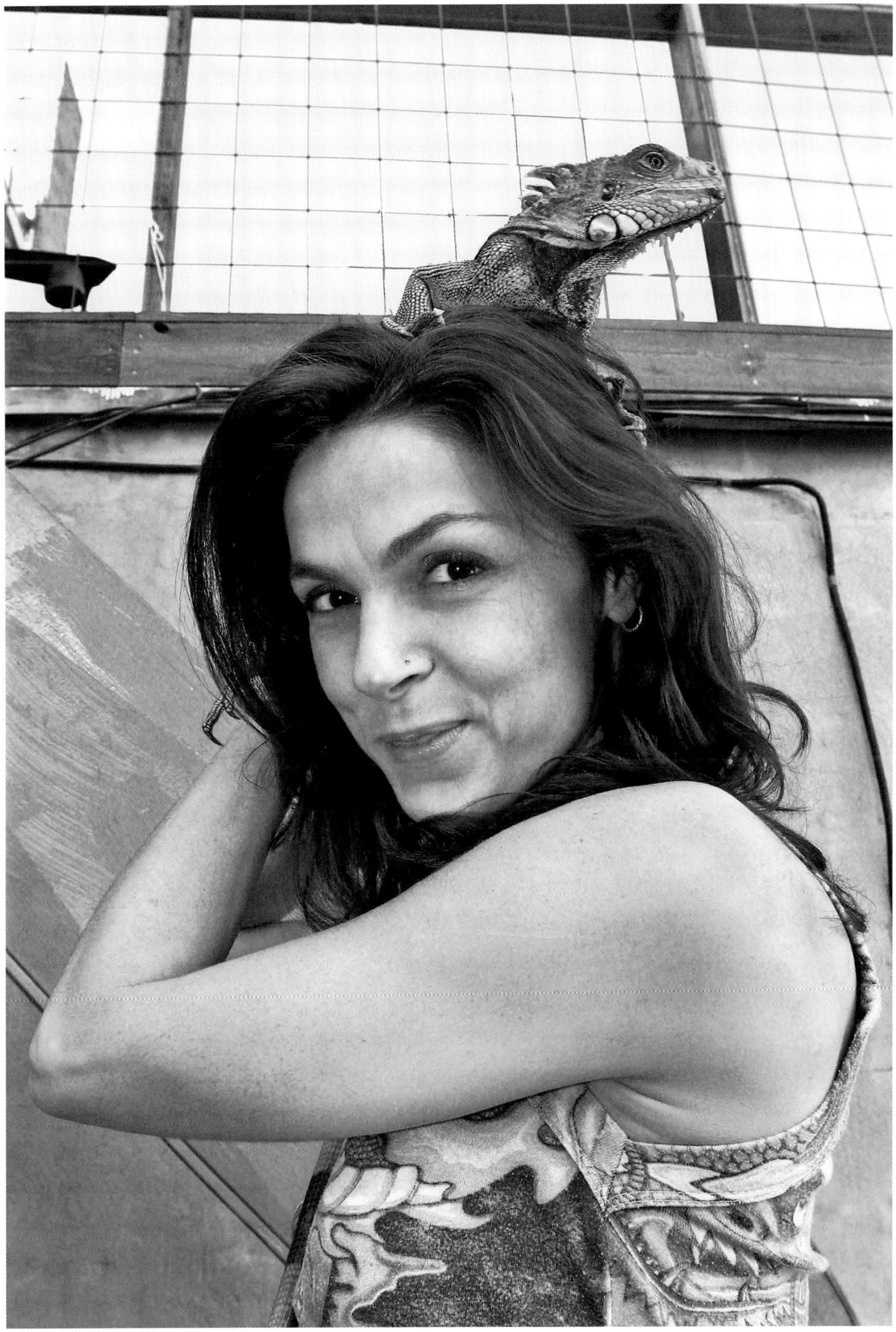

Irving Layton in his room
at Maimonides Geriatric Centre, Côte-St-Luc, November 2000

When I visited Irving Layton at Maimonides, he looked as vigorous and as leonine as he had for decades. However, age had laid its claim on him. He was tended by two bustling women, one large and suspicious and the other, Musia, rake-thin, colourfully dressed, and irrepressibly lively. Irving smiled, nodded, returned my greeting, and said almost nothing else. Musia slyly broke the silence as I photographed by repeating the opening words of one of Layton's poems. On hearing the familiar line he immediately threw his chest out and declaimed the rest of the poem. After that, silence. Toward the end of our meeting, Irving suddenly spoke to Musia. "What happened to all those pretty young girls who used to follow me around?" he asked. Musia looked at once dubious and amused, then said, "They got old, Irving. They got old!" When I left the room, a very old lady sitting in a wheelchair immediately outside Irving's room spoke anxiously to me. "Did you see Irving?" she asked. "Did you see the poet?"

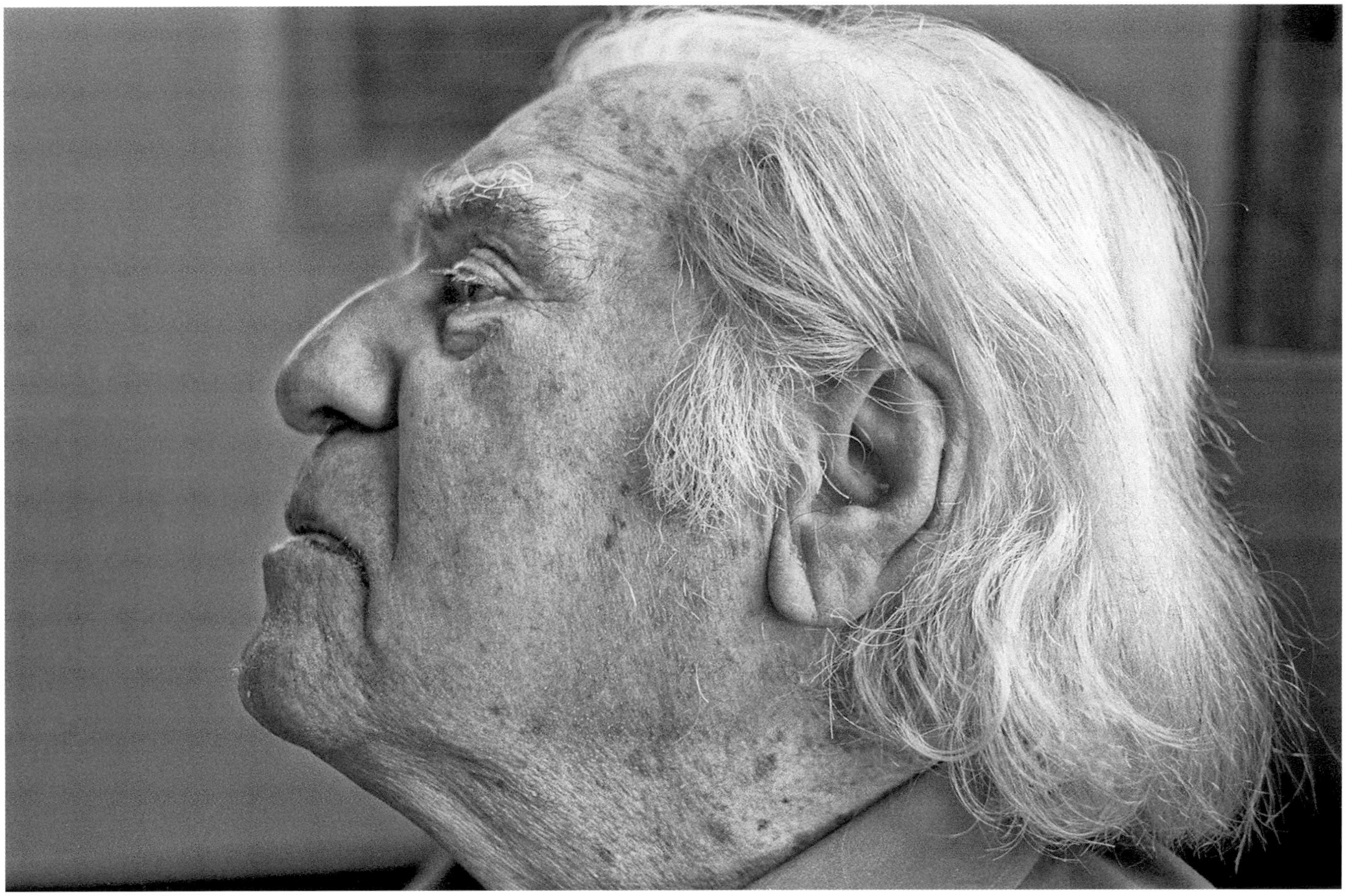

Norm Sibum in the stairwell

outside his Sherbrooke Street apartment, Notre-Dame-de-Grâce, November 2007

As I killed a few minutes outside Norm Sibum's apartment building, waiting for our appointment, a man wearing a fleece zip-up and sporting extravagantly bushy eyebrows under a flat grey cap walked past me and into the building with the faintest hint of wariness. A few minutes later, I rang and the same man, Norm Sibum, introduced himself in an offhanded manner and showed me into a small apartment whose walls were crowded with paintings by his friendly and garrulous partner. Norm was an American who had come to Canada in that wave of politically unhappy immigrants who, as it often happened, were distressed to discover that Canada was not always just like home. Norm was contending with far more than the experience of being an immigrant, though. He talked about social class in general and what might be taken for a class structure within the world of poets. Somehow, we found ourselves in the stairwell with his partner, who was equally vexed about the art world and its preference for theory over craft. While she spoke, Norm was quiet and seemed quite happy to sit in the background, as though the expression of resentment was, itself, fatiguing.

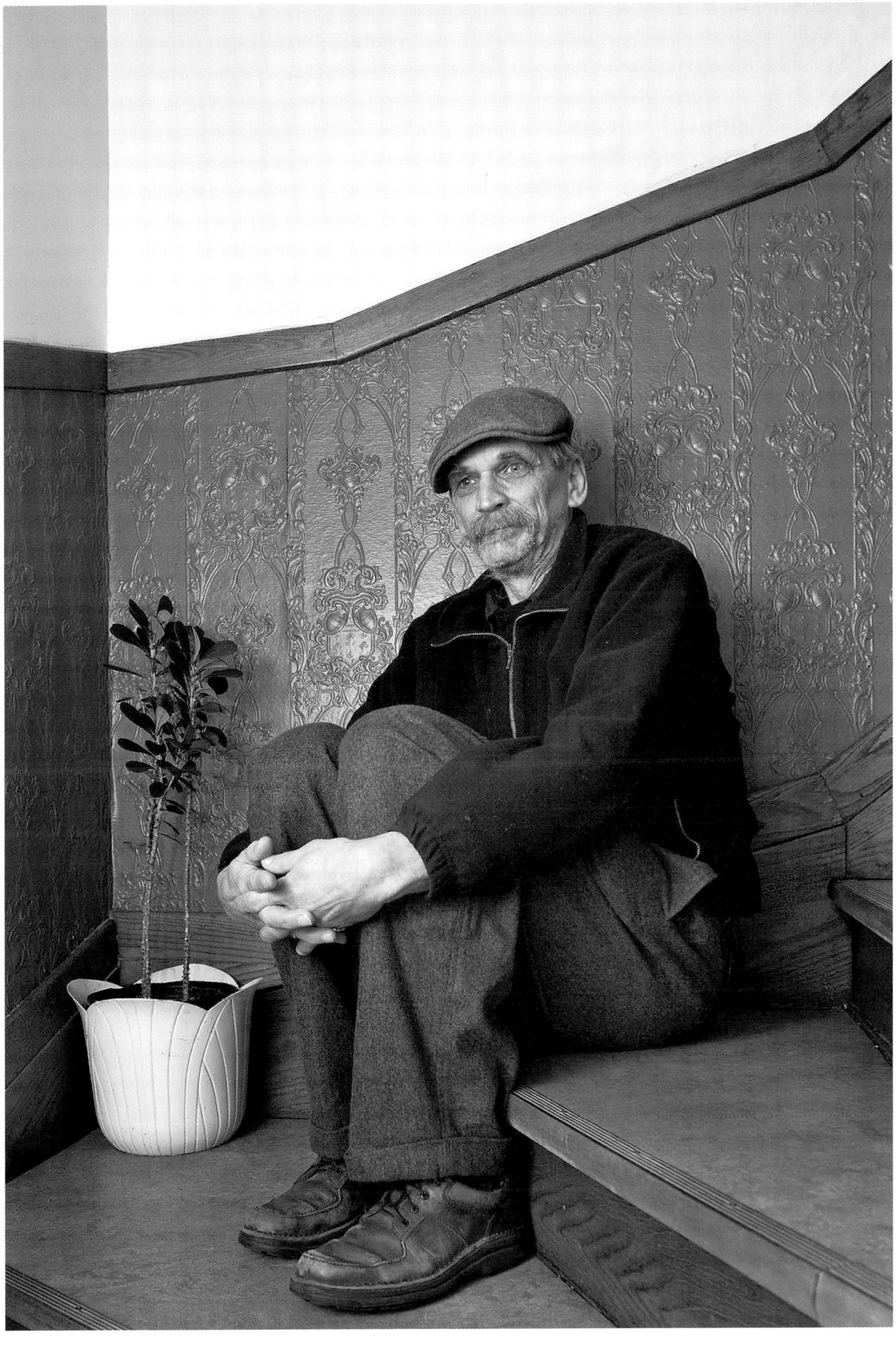

Susan Gillis in her apartment
on Melrose Avenue in Notre-Dame-de-Grâce, July 2002

I had met Susan when she was a graduate student, but we had to negotiate a new relation to each other as photographer and subject. The photographer is almost always an interloper, and that position can feel exaggerated when the subject is a woman in her home and no one else is present. Susan was noticeably guarded at first, but she displayed a natural physical poise. As we talked, we began to trade stories about the ways we had consciously departed from the sound and look of the places where we had grown up. Susan spoke about the gradual changes in her Nova Scotia accent that made her sound less "regional." I couldn't hear the smallest hint of Atlantic coast in her speech. She never entirely relaxed in front of the camera, but she didn't need to. Some subjects translate their lack of ease into postures that put them at odds with their environments. Susan merely adopted the contours of hers.

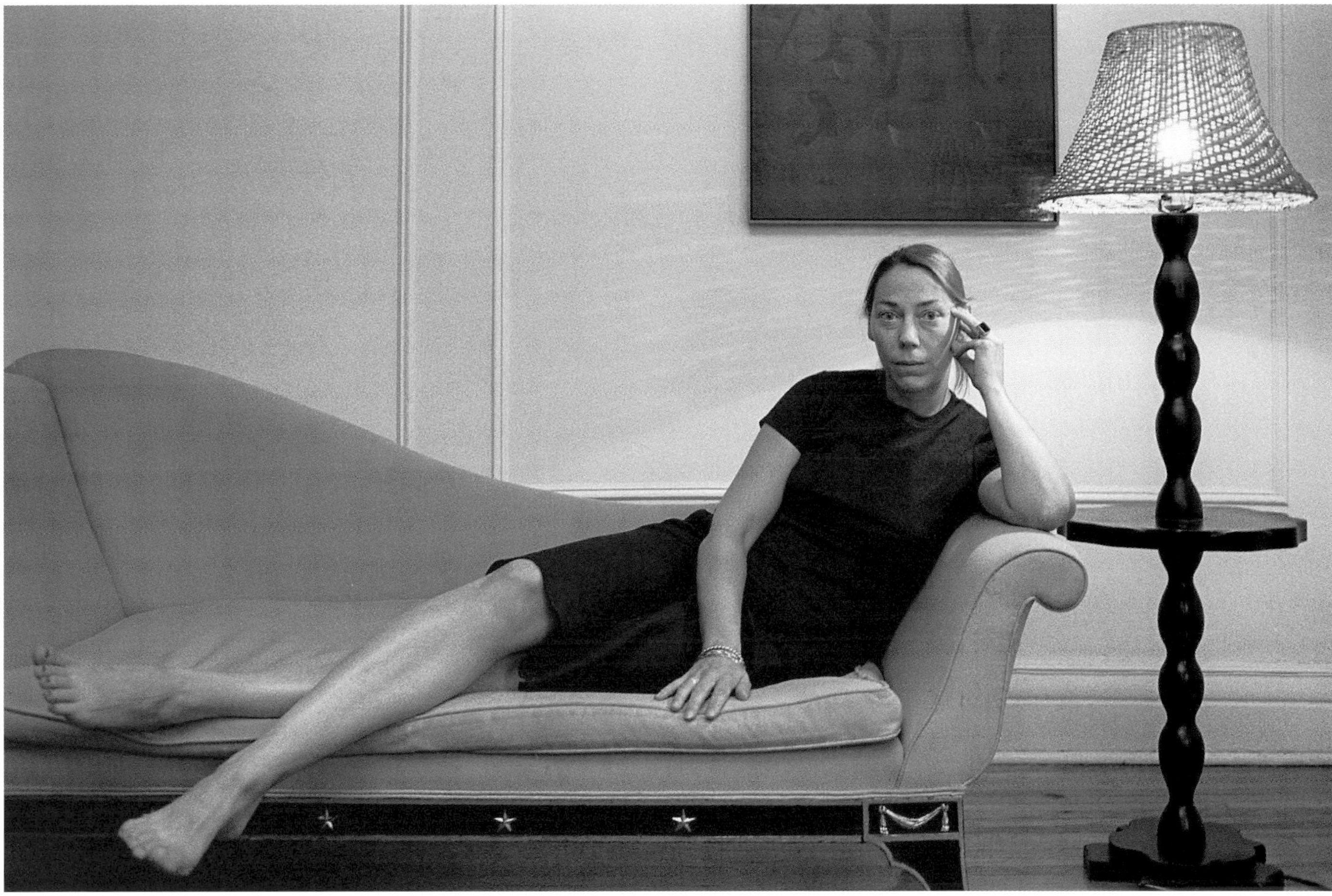

Glen Rotchin in the basement of 99 Chabanel, Montreal, March 2005

A STOOPED YOUNG MAN with ear locks and a yarmulke that was slightly askew nodded in greeting and went to collect his boss when I entered the door of Glen Rotchin's offices in a building that had once been the centre of the garment industry in Canada. Glen's grandfather, a pioneer in the industry, had leased an entire floor of the building, where he manufactured clothing. Now, Glen worked as the building manager, overseeing its transition to a different sort of economy. We trudged up and down flight after flight—to the basement, to the snowy, gravelled roof, to the room where the elevators were controlled by clicking antique relays and solenoids. Glen took evident, boyish pleasure in each of these places he had known since childhood. That pleasure soured a little when we visited an empty manufacturing room where scores of bales of abandoned fabric were stacked in front of bare work tables. However, it returned in the basement, where the carcasses of old machinery sat abandoned on concrete pedestals and Glen moved among them with the same sense of delight he must have felt as a boy.

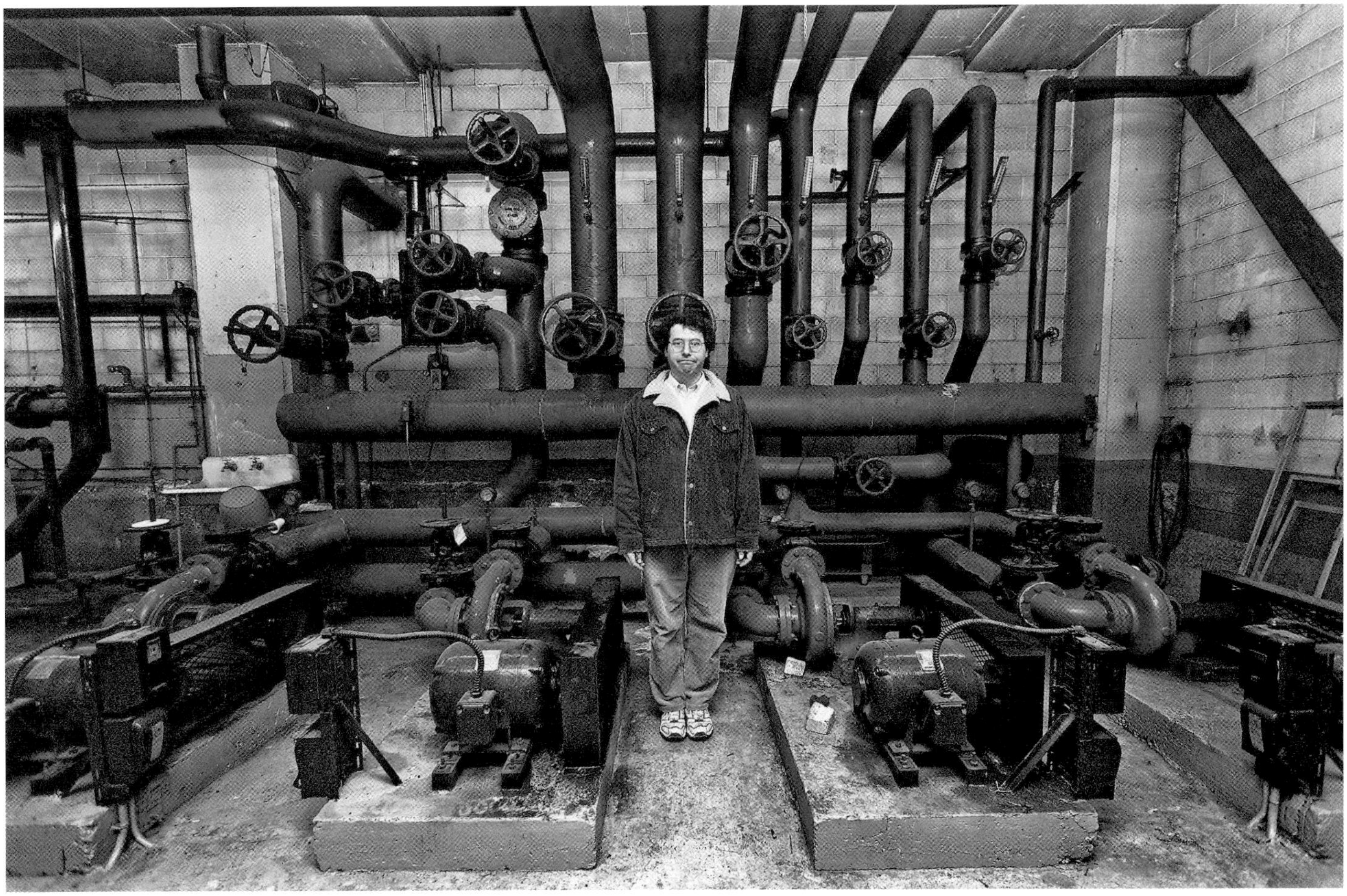

MADELEINE THIEN AT A WESTMOUNT HOME ON ARLINGTON AVENUE, MARCH 2006

MADDIE THIEN WAS NOT EVEN CLOSE TO HOME when this photograph was made. Her family was from Malaysia but she grew up in Vancouver, moved to Holland with her Dutch husband, and then settled in Quebec City, where he conducted research in robotics. She told me that where she lived in Holland, people spoke Frisian—not one of her languages—so her life was one of relative solitude. In Quebec City, she was working to improve her French. Despite that, some people made the assumption she was far from home ground and approached her to comment on her hair or ask where she was from. It's a commonplace to say that writers are comfortable not feeling entirely accepted or at home anywhere, and may even prefer the extra clarity that outsider status grants them. Yet, it was hard not to wonder about the point at which one feels less like a watchful bystander and more like an isolated object of curiosity.

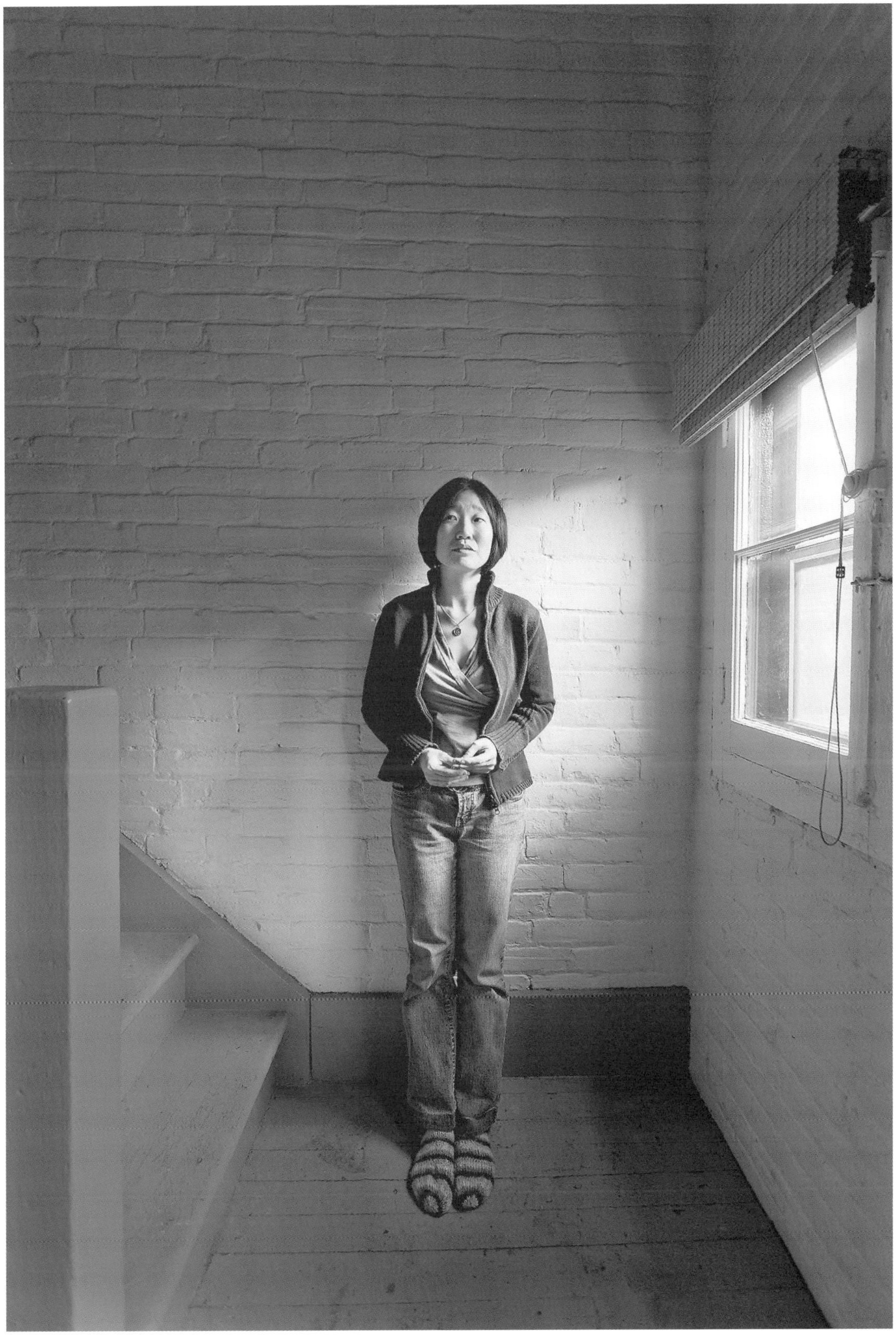

Rawi Hage on the roof
of his apartment building in Côte-des-Neiges, December 2007

SLIPPERY WINTER SLUSH greeted me on the long walk from a métro station to Rawi Hage's apartment building near St. Justine Hospital. Rawi, wearing a black tuque and blue jeans, showed me in and offered tea. I declined, but he offered it again a few minutes later, apologetically explaining, "Maybe it's my cultural background, but I want to be a good host." The walls of his apartment were lively with paintings—of sinking ships in a white sea, a loose-haired young girl wearing a T-shirt, an athletic boy riding an abstract shape below a snaking red line. The largest was lit with a photographer's incandescent "hot light" on a light stand. Before becoming a writer, Rawi had been a photographer and visual artist. He also did the journeyman work of photographing everything from weddings to construction sites. Before leaving, I asked if any of the paintings on display were his. He looked a little pained and amused and gestured toward a dark, geometrical design facing his front door. "That one," he said, his head bobbing self-consciously, "but it's really not very good."

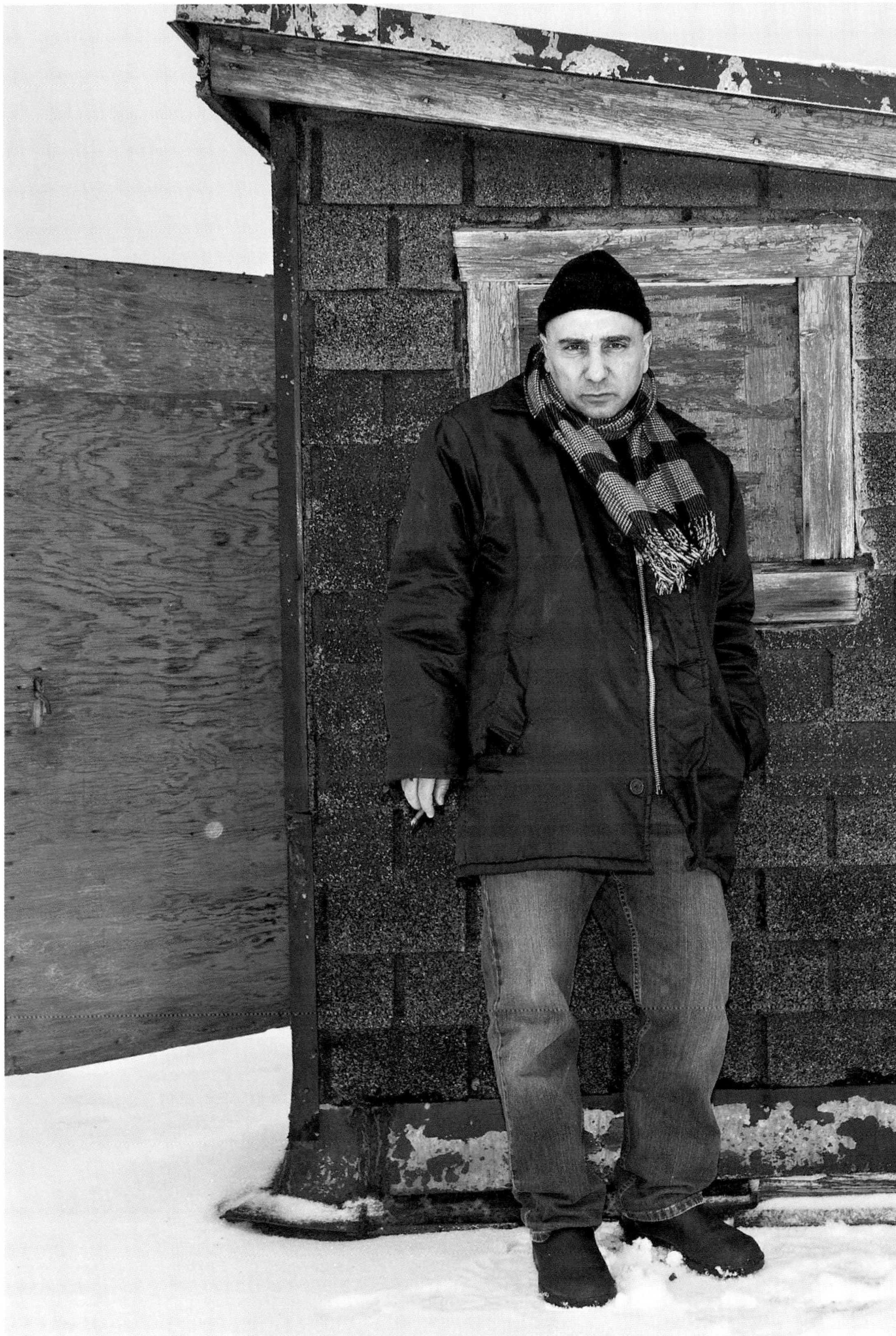

Kaie Kellough in the front room of his home on rue Hochelaga, Montreal, April 2008

FIVE YEARS TO THE DAY before this image was made, I had photographed a very reserved Kaie Kellough DJing his weekly show at McGill University's radio station. When I visited him in the apartment he and his wife had just purchased in east-end Montreal, he was apologetic about our earlier shoot and forthright about himself. He is from Vancouver by way of Alberta but works in French, explaining that he was a "Trudeau-era kid" who received his west-coast education in French. He follows boxing, was delighted when I suggested that he download a recent CBC interview with Angelo Dundee, Muhammad Ali's corner man, and told me examples of boxers who suffered from *dementia pugilistica* because of the repeated concussions they had received. He loves boogie-woogie piano players like Memphis Slim, who sing as well as play. He showed me clippings about the British dub poet Benjamin Zephaniah, who turned down an OBE. He affectionately told me about his wife, a Boston jazz singer and practitioner of yoga whose tongue has difficulty with Québec French. He made the observation that writers are too intensely witty and competitive to be cool and that musicians are too cool and laid back to be witty. The rabbit, by the way, is named "Mr. B" and, according to Kaie, "has all his parts" and doesn't bite.

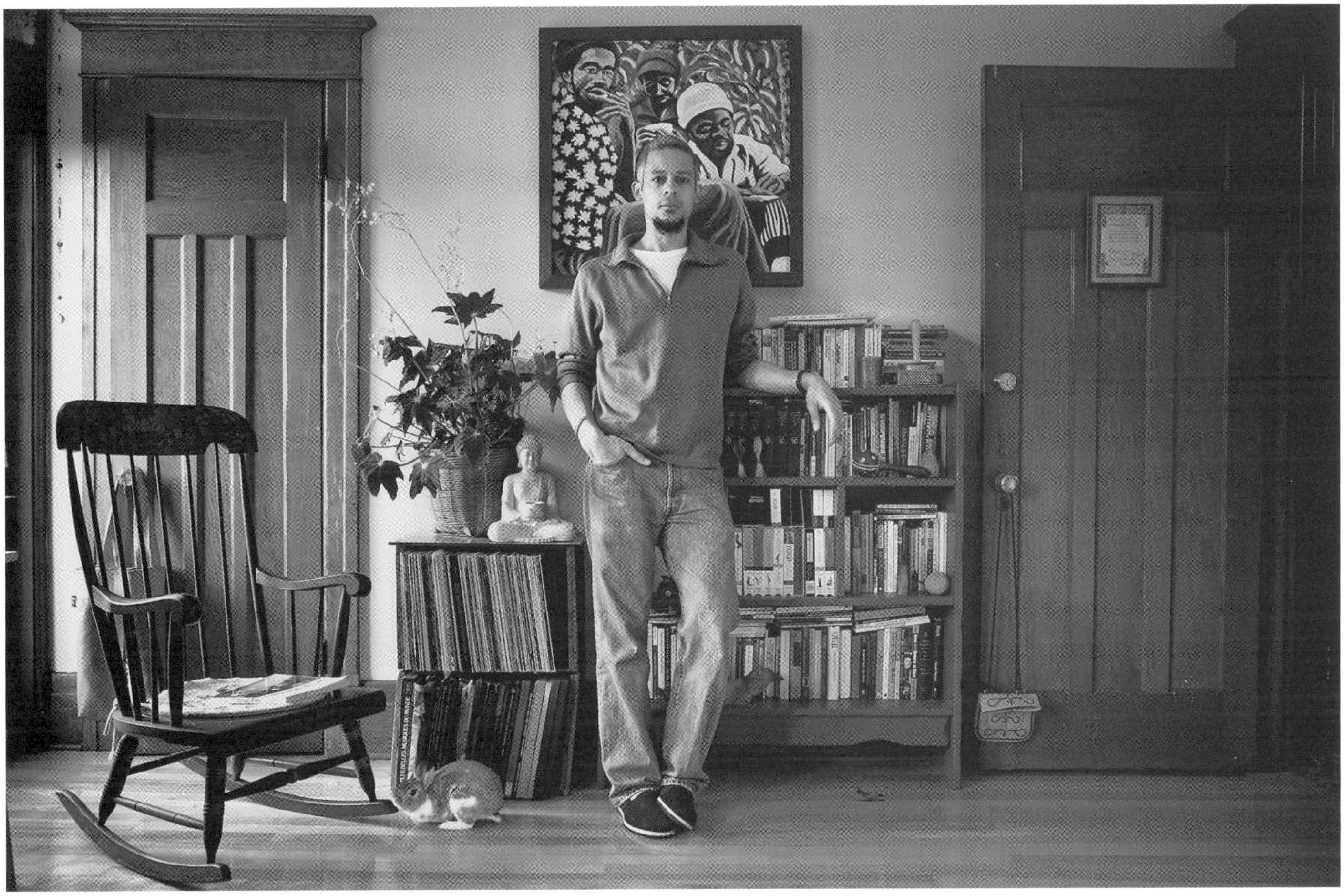

STEPHANIE BOLSTER IN HER RUE MARCIL APARTMENT, NOTRE-DAME-DE-GRÂCE, FEBRUARY 2002

STEPHANIE WROTE LATE INTO THE NIGHT, and we avoided scheduling an early shoot for that reason. The art that decorated her apartment—including a green Barbotine-ware plate, a dark blue Limoges box, paintings of Vancouver and Québec, Victorian prints, and a Lemieux poster—suggested less the sensibility of a curator or collector than that of someone with an incredibly keen eye for modest beauty. When we began to make photographs, I was curious to see if she would want to direct me and to control the content of each frame. Instead, she was interested in hearing about the ways people saw themselves in photographs. When we talked about the nature—or even the problem—of beauty, I told her that two of my female subjects had asked me to photograph them nude because, as one had said, "Art is long, beauty is short." She did not respond to this story right away, making me anxious that, in the odd frontier of intimacy, trust, and formality between a female subject and a male photographer, I had trespassed in some way. However, after we finished, she had two comments. One was a worry that she had looked tired after an exceptionally late writing night, and the other was an expression of gratitude for my anecdotes about women, beauty, and photographs.

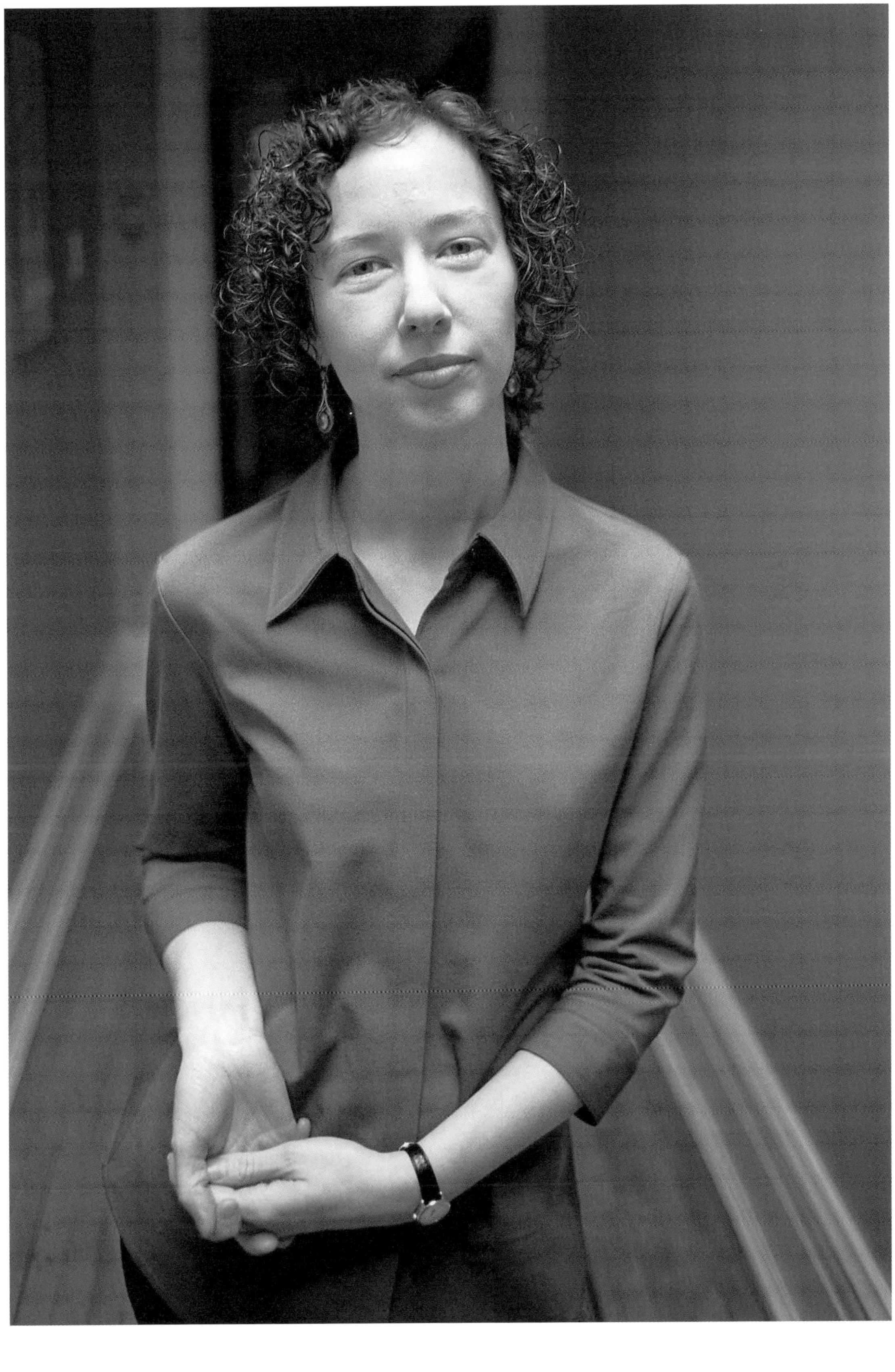

Bakhyt Kenjeev in his apartment on Park Avenue, Mile End, December 2007

BAKHYT KENJEEV, whose parents were ethnic Kazakhs, had been described to me as one of the best living Russian-language poets, yet no local writers outside the community of Russian speakers in Montreal had heard of him. I had seen him briefly at a party attended by many Russians, and they moved around him in a curious way, as though his mere presence distorted gravity in the room. When I entered his apartment, in the early afternoon, he stood facing me with his hands on the back of a kitchen chair. "The first thing you must understand," he said, looking over the top of his glasses, "is that this is a Russian household. We drink." With that, he produced a tall, narrow bottle and three shot glasses. The third glass was for another Russian writer, who was late joining us. The instant Bakhyt tilted the bottle over the first glass, the telephone rang. He looked up, pretending annoyance. "That idiot," he said. "He knows we are drinking and wants us to wait." He was right; the other writer arrived within minutes. Throughout the afternoon, the Soviet Union lay just under the surface of every topic, whether it was language, art, or sex. Bakhyt took me through the rooms of his small apartment and displayed plaster busts of icons that the Soviets used to instill a sense of duty in its civilians. One was the head of a soldier with notably bland features, who symbolized service and sacrifice. After showing off this sample of totalitarian kitsch, Bakhyt replaced it on his bookshelf with inexplicable, wry tenderness.

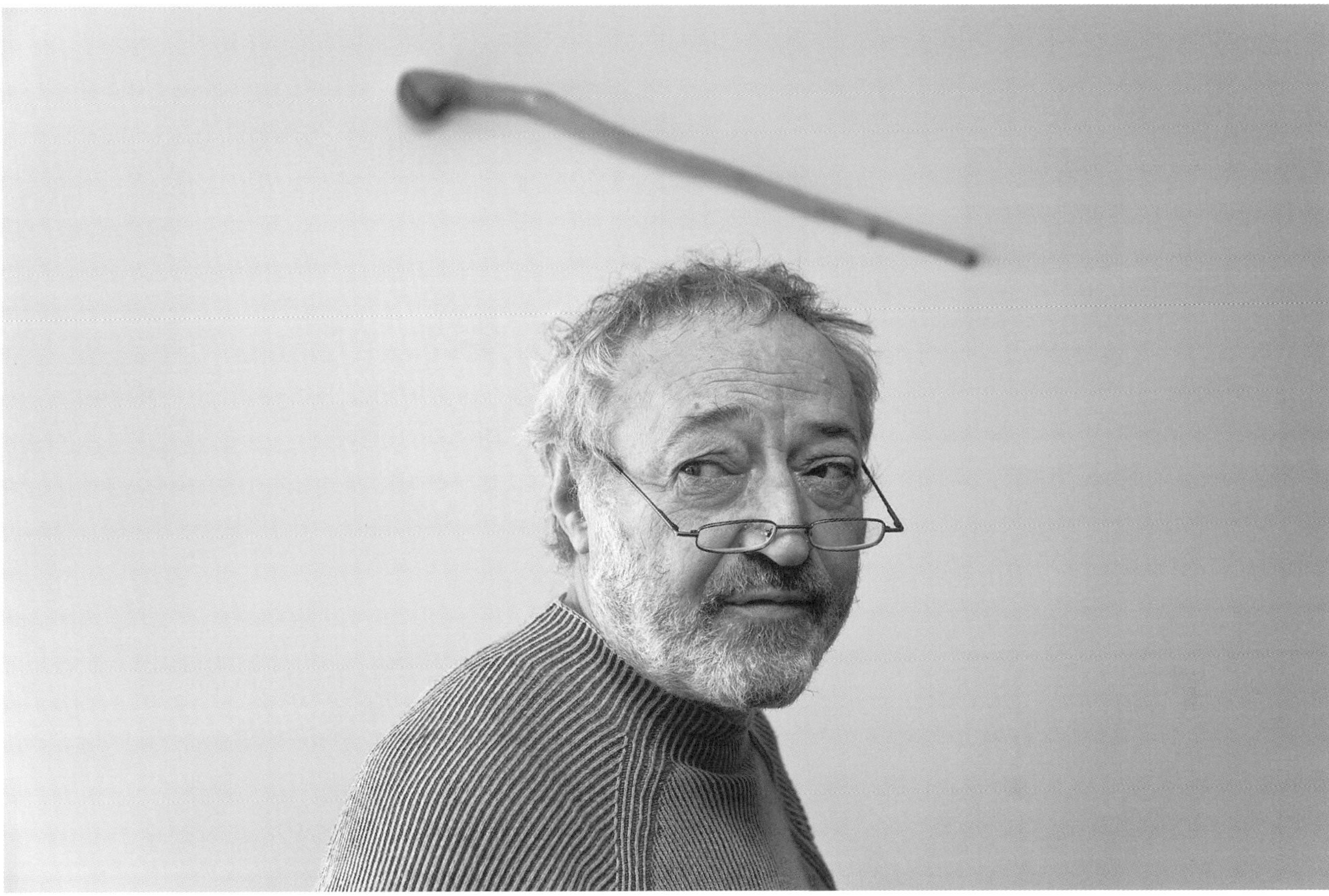

Robert Allen in his loft
on rue Notre Dame on the edge of Old Montreal, October 1998

ROBERT DIED OF CANCER eight years after this photograph was made. The story I heard, but have not verified, is that he was in England when he received an urgent call confirming a diagnosis of malignant melanoma on his scalp. The terrible urgency of this situation stood in contrast with the way he lived. Robert seemed always to take the path of least resistance, exemplifying cool, and valuing imagination and invention more than order. He travelled frequently and extensively in the U.S., the country whose popular culture and literature he chose as his imaginative homeland. A friend of Robert's told me about road trips they had taken in a convertible. It seems likely that long days spent driving under the southern sun that nourished him also brought him harm. When I photographed him, there was not yet a whisper of his problem. Here, he donned his dark glasses and his hand flew to his chin as though two images—the august literary presence and the hipster—had simultaneously taken command of his self-image.

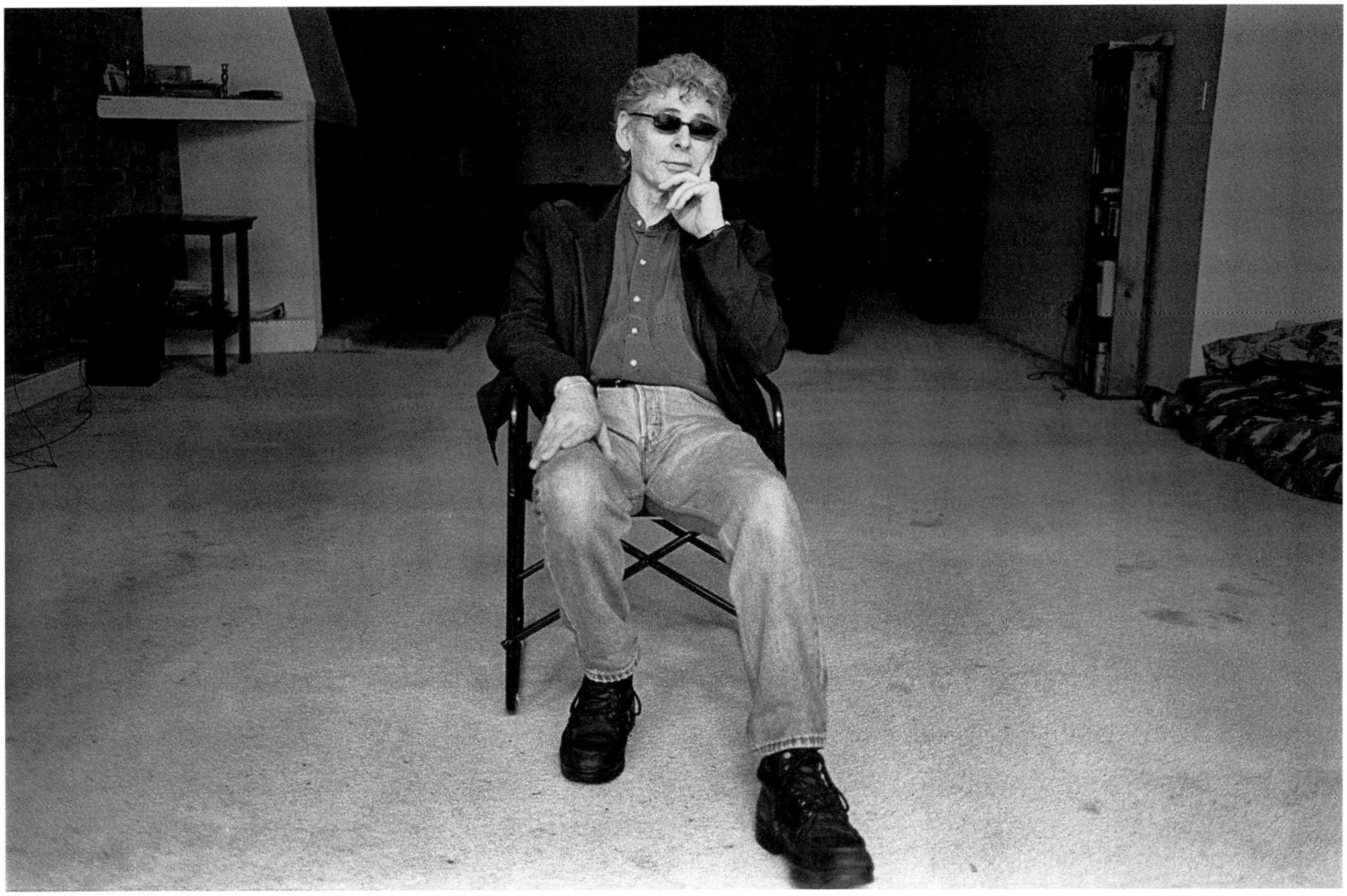

Anita Rau Badami in her home on rue Terrebonne in Notre-Dame-de-Grâce, May 2003

Anita was unfailingly cheery and sociable, and promptly forgot the camera as she talked about writers and writing. We took photographs in almost every room in her large house, barring the one her mother-in-law was staying in. Although she knew that we weren't trying to make an entirely conventional literary portrait, she asked if she could submit some of these images to her publisher for use on the jacket of her latest book. When the time came, Anita did choose a few and sent them to her publisher. They were rejected as not being "sexy" enough, and the publisher dispatched a photographer to make a new portrait. In these, she appeared heavy-lidded and shared the frame with Hindu religious icons. "And we're not even religious!" she said.

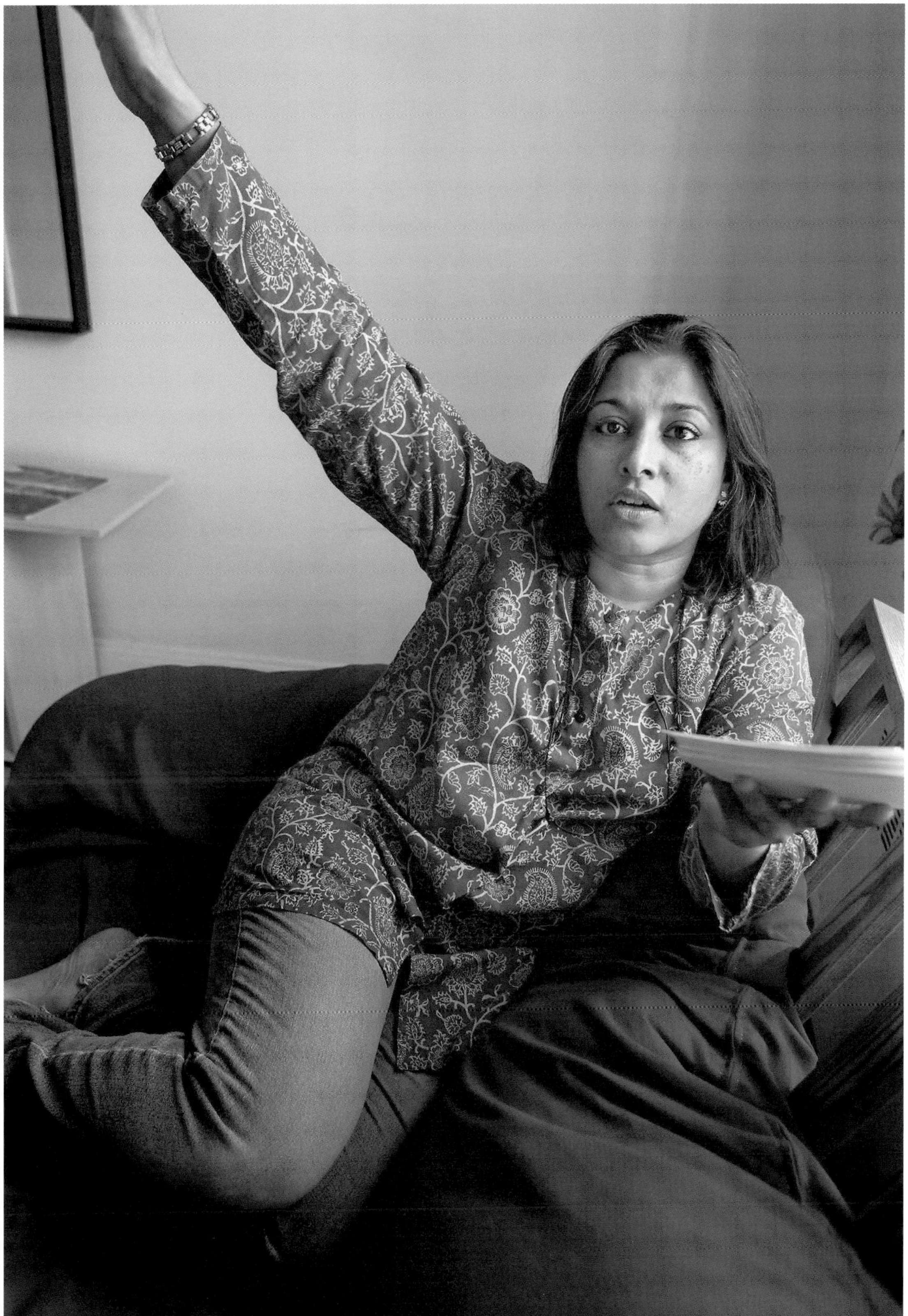

Steve Galluccio in the conference room of l'Agence Goodwin in Montreal, March 2008

I met Steve Galluccio in a meticulously restored nineteenth-century mansion on Sherbrooke Street in the east end of Montreal. The frosted glass doors on the ground floor were posted with a hand-written sign warning "*Tournage*"—filming in progress—so I crept up the curving wooden staircase to find Steve chatting with his agent. The only space available to us was a conference room, which looked drearily like a conference room. Steve told me that his home in Little Italy was off limits to photographers and interviewers, that it was a private place. As we talked, he seemed almost uninterested in our meeting. However, I did pique him when I asked about another Italian-Canadian screenwriter who wrote gangster films. "I don't touch that!" he said, making a face. He professed an affinity for Latin cultures, or, in the case of Quebec, self-declared Latin cultures. Toronto, he felt, was all grey order, lack of spirit, and slavish imitation of American style. Montreal, on the other hand, was part of Canada in name only, and a better and more adventurous world for artists. Just before I left, I eavesdropped on a conversation he had with the lively receptionist at L'Agence Goodwin. He was explaining his feelings about the privacy of his home to her. "Just as well," she said, in crisply perfect French. "It's not very nice!"

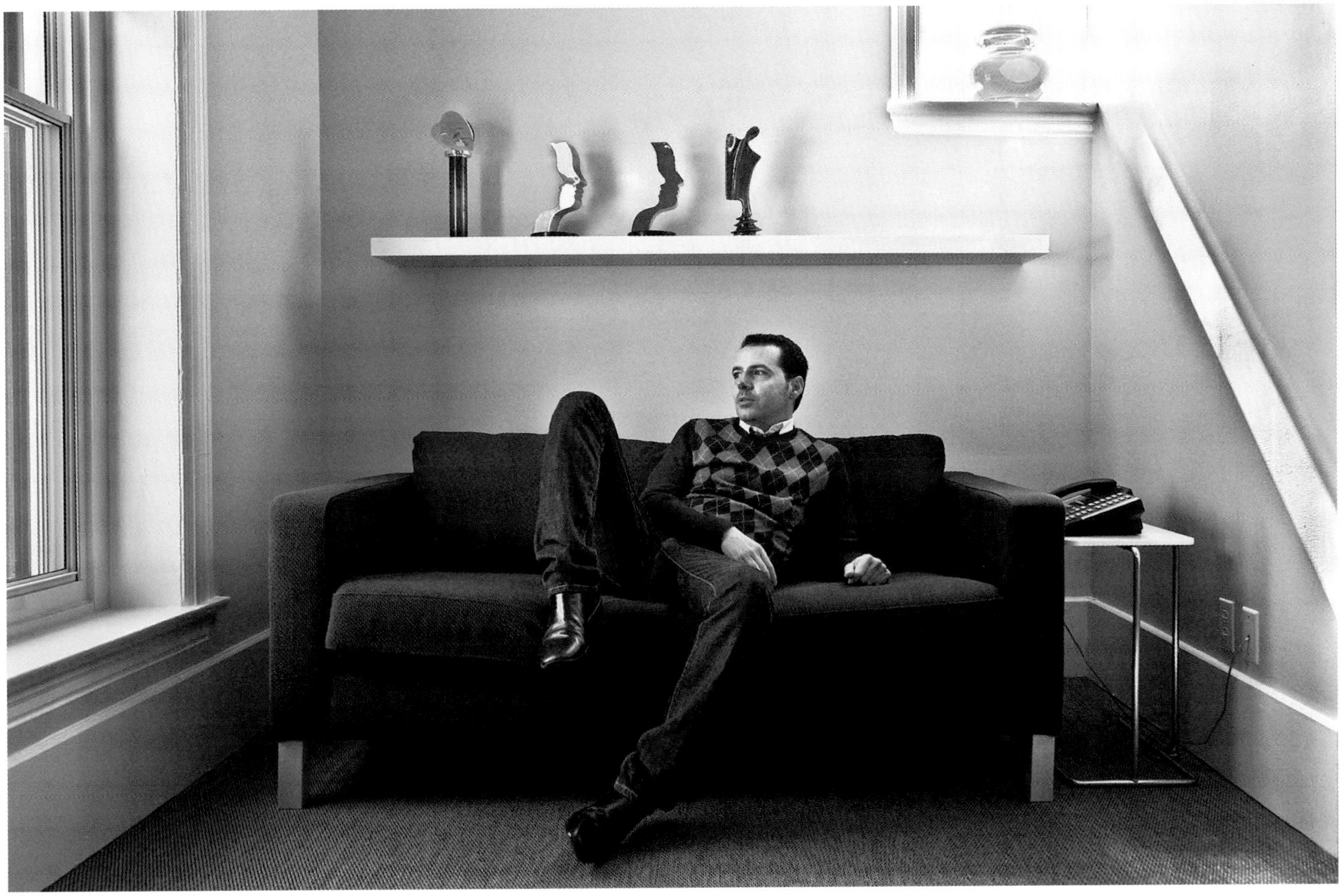

JOHN MCAULEY OUTSIDE HIS APARTMENT BUILDING ON LINCOLN AVENUE, MONTREAL, OCTOBER 2003

I HAD KNOWN JOHN MCAULEY for some years before this photograph was made, sometimes encountering him at a copy centre as he turned the pages of German or French books about lighter-than-air machines. He had been a member of the Vehicule group of poets many years before, but I thought of him as the man giving painful and extended birth to the world's definitive history of blimps and zeppelins. However, when I visited him for this photograph, John was filled with new enthusiasm for his poetry, and was writing and publishing. He showed me shelves in a tall closet stacked with old manuscripts and those under revision, and it was evident that something had come back to life for him. The zeppelins—or at least the history surrounding them—were still aloft in both our imaginations, though, and returned in a discussion of military history. At that point, John showed me a defunct World War I German hand grenade. It looked so fragile and its parts were so loose-fitting that the past it represented seemed both harmless and irrecoverable.

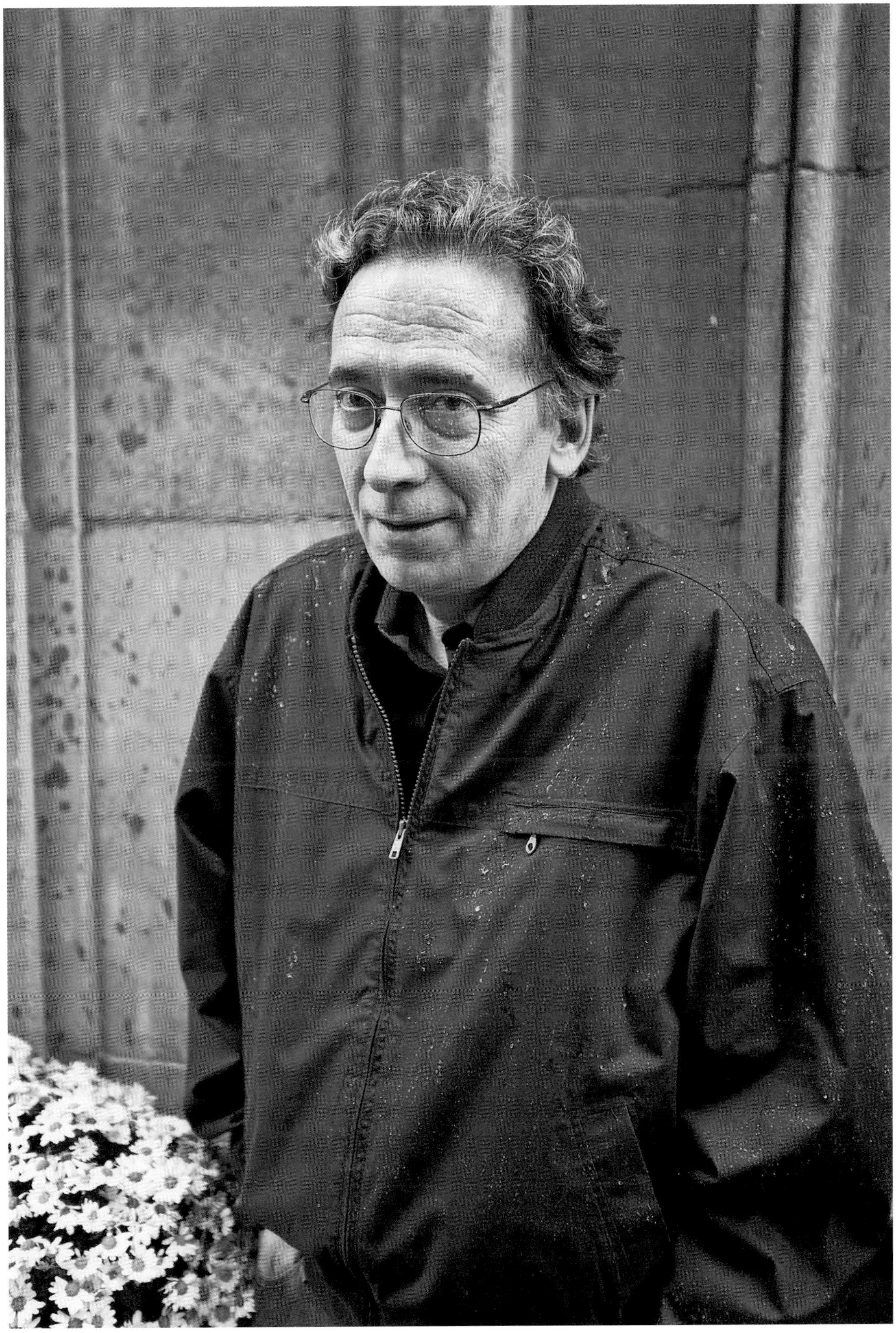

Claire Rothman in her music room, Westmount, April 2003

Claire's home is a trek up a hill whose steep incline once represented both the topography and the class structure of Montreal. Nearby streets like Prince Albert, Windsor, Victoria, and Chesterfield have names that speak of the neighbourhood's history. The photographs I made included a stately portrait of Claire in front of her fireplace, but it was the kind of image one might want to hang in a hall of ancestors. When we finished, I asked her if there were a setting she wanted to be photographed in, and she immediately sank to the floor, her legs folded beneath her, and grinned. "Here," she said. "This is the way I feel comfortable." When I first met Claire she was working as a waitress, articling in a law firm to complete her legal training, and finishing a book of stories with settings that included rural Guyana and small-town Quebec. She is a subject who is never completely contextualized by her environment.

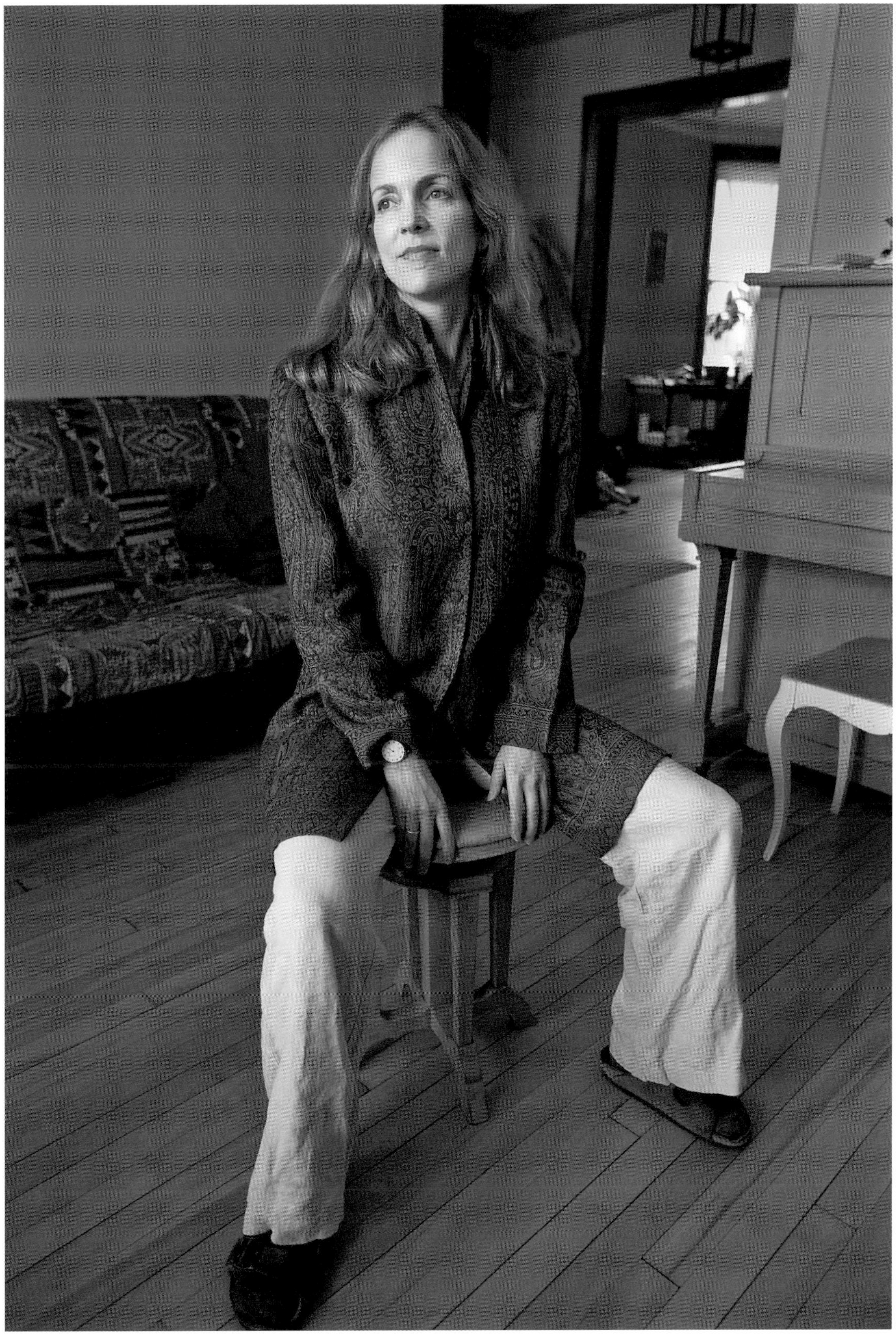

Denise Roig on her apartment balcony, Connaught Avenue, Notre-Dame-de-Grâce, August 2000

DENISE'S DAUGHTER saw a performance of Cirque du Soleil in Los Angeles, where she and Denise lived, and conceived the idea that she would like to become a circus performer. Bravely, the two set off for Montreal in the hope that she would be able to enroll in the circus school on Sherbrooke Street but found themselves instead in the small city of Sherbrooke in the Eastern Townships. They did manage to sort out the place names, and found their way to Montreal. When I photographed her, Denise—as open and as trusting a subject as I've had—became a little reserved and self-protective only when she told me about her perplexity at having discovered the unquestioning reverence in which a few Canadian writers were held, and the chumminess created by a grant-supported culture. She had been prepared to find her way in a new country, but the sanctity of its artists and the critical establishment that supported them presented a new and difficult cultural geography.

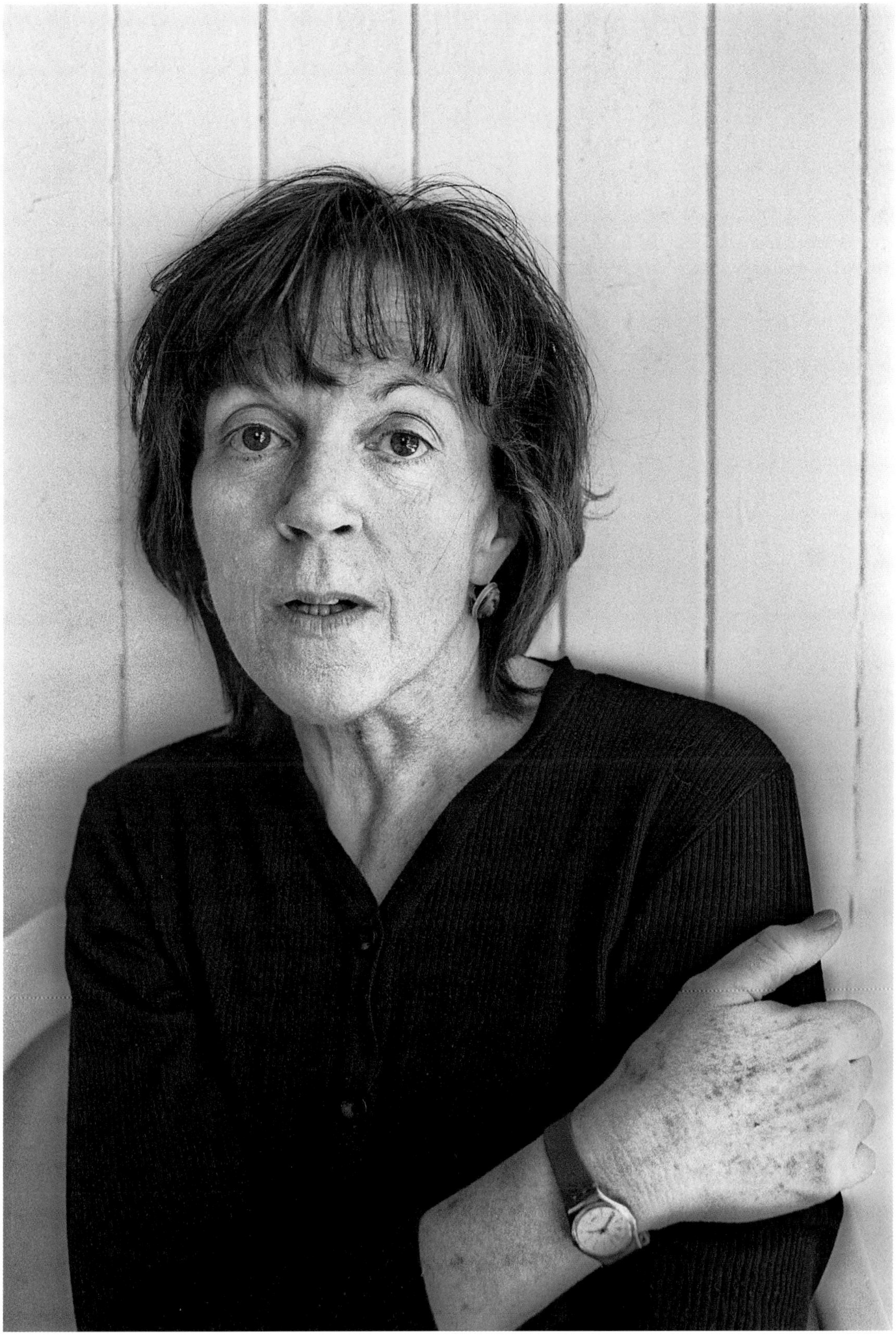

Taras Grescoe in his apartment
on rue Bernard in Outremont, March 2003

Taras's apartment looked like a parody of a travel writer's home. An unruly pile of cardboard boxes was gathered in the entranceway. The walls were bare except for an occasional ornament that looked like a placeholder for the possibility of a more permanent decoration. CDs sat in a tall and very unstable stack near a stereo on the floor. The bookcases, however, were orderly, and revealed an interest in odd bits of the world that would never occur to an ordinary traveller. Taras himself was certainly no ordinary traveller. He had recently published a book on Quebec—subtitled *An Unsentimental Journey Through Quebec*—that had earned him the ire of those with a more sentimental notion of the province. His ideas about travel seemed to have at least as much to do with travellers as with place and he told amusing and sometimes mildly scornful anecdotes about them. Toward the end of our time, he rummaged through one of the many boxes in the apartment and produced a photograph he had taken of western travellers in Nepal standing on a high plateau with their tiny cameras all raised toward the climbing sun. In Taras's photograph, there was no splashy sunrise, though, only foreigners trying to reify their experience of foreigness by embalming it in a snapshot.

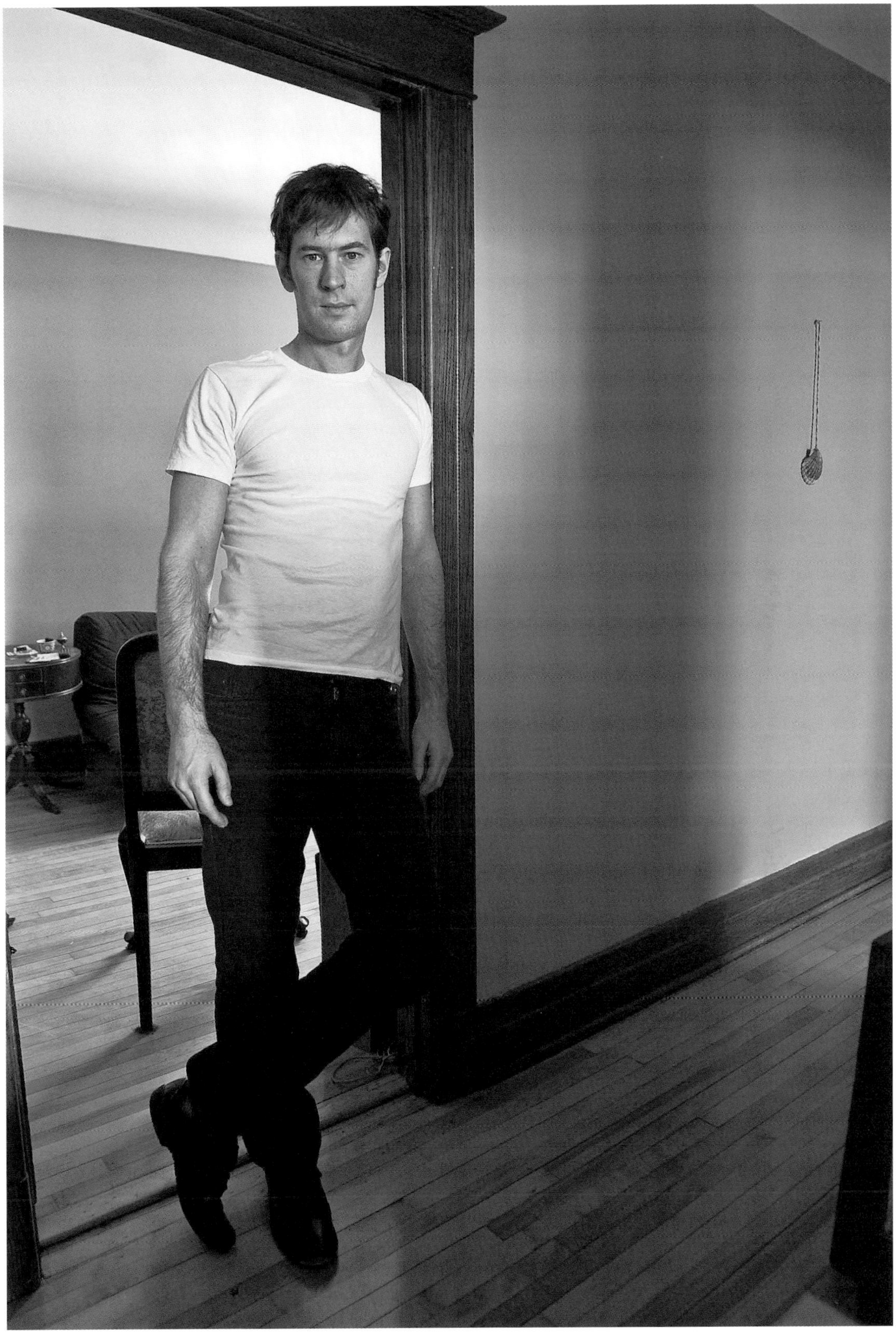

ROBYN SARAH IN THE ENTRANCE TO HER HOME ON RUE HUTCHISON, PLATEAU MONT-ROYAL, OCTOBER 2000

ROBYN MET ME ON THE WAY to one of her favourite walking paths on wooded Mount Royal. The first snow had yet to fall and the mountain looked bare. Robyn's husband is a distinguished photographer who travelled throughout North Africa photographing ancient and abandoned Jewish sites. Possibly because she was with me, Robyn stopped at a badly weathered stone fountain and speculated on the way her husband would photograph it. She also told me about his allergy to photographic chemicals, his extraordinary ability to "read" a negative, and a recent edition of prints. As for our own picture-taking, the options were not very promising: leafless, wooded settings are a jumble of lines that grow over and around the human shape. The mountain trail was not endless, though, and we ended our walk at her home. "I might like a copy of the print," Robyn said, when we had finished. "My husband insists on getting everything just right, so I don't even have a publicity photo."

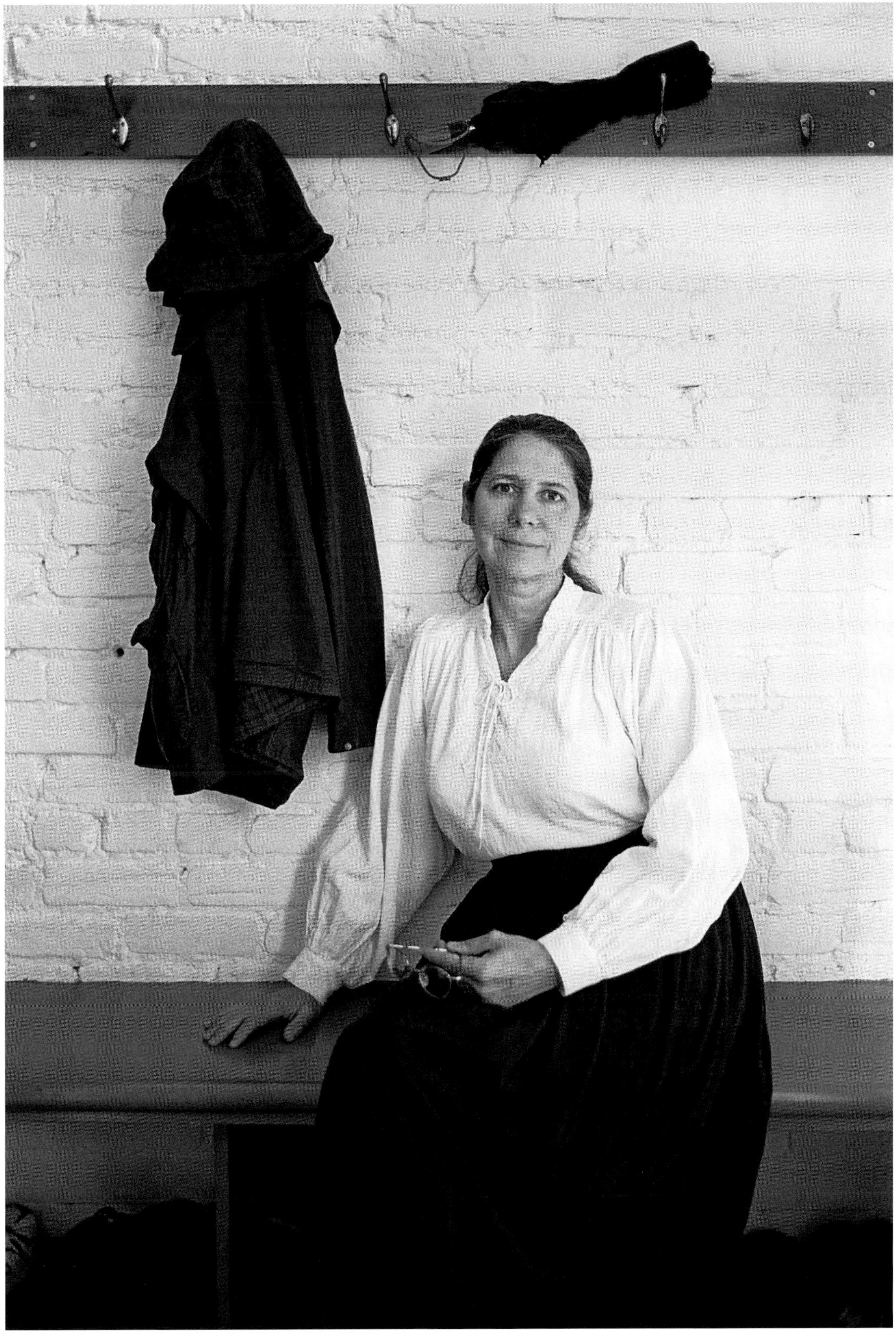

GEOFFREY COOK, NEWLY MOVED IN,
RUE GILFORD, PLATEAU MONT-ROYAL, JULY 2004

GEOFF AND HIS WIFE were recently married and had merged households, and space in their elegant but small rooms looked a little tight. The kitchen table was crowded with clay-potted plants, a watermelon, and the spilled contents of one of those ubiquitous kitchen drawers that hold everything from keys to drill bits to dental floss. Geoff, barefoot, sat down and absent-mindedly pieced through the collection. In a few minutes, we shifted location to a rooftop patio, where he showed me a rough-hewn wooden table that he said he had made with only one tool—a pocket knife—during a particularly boring stay in his home province of Nova Scotia. Geoff's wife, a vivacious Afghan woman who had worked for the U.N. in Afghanistan as a food security advisor, came home near the end of our session. Geoff asked if I would take a picture of them together. It was the only image he wanted a copy of.

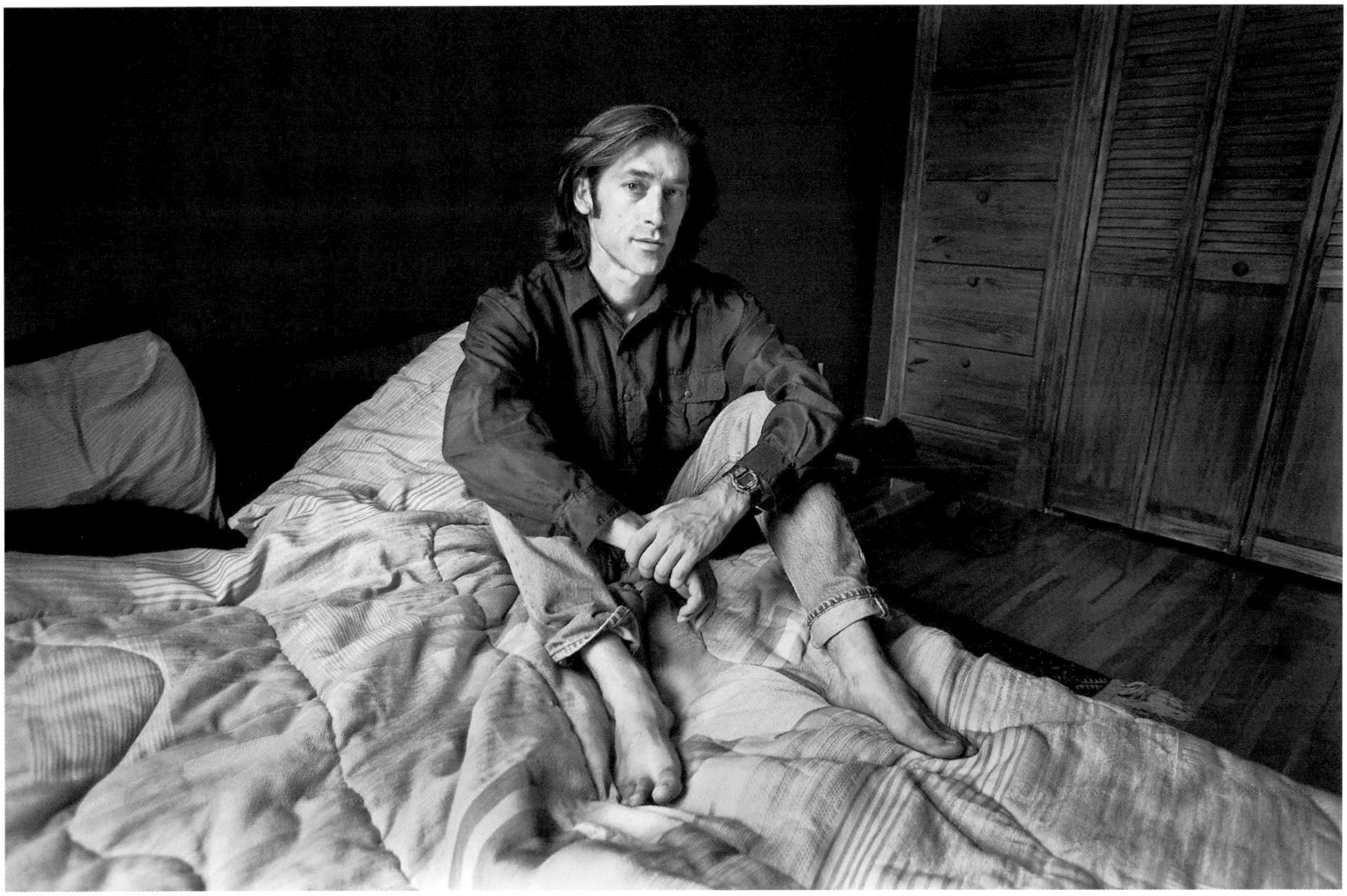

Carmine Starnino in a parking lot in Little Italy, October 2000

We met first in Carmine's apartment, the basement of his uncle's duplex in Little Italy. The apartment was one of the least inhabited-looking places I've seen. It contained the obvious accoutrements of an ordinary life, like basic furniture and clothing, but there was little in the way of decoration, no sign of food or cooking, and absolutely no evidence that it had ever seen a visitor before me. As Carmine paged through a long essay on poetry he was completing, plucking out ideas that were elegantly argued and sometimes contentious, I understood that his work was his home. We took a walk through Little Italy and visited Nostra Madonna della Difesa church, on whose dome Carmine pointed out a pre-war painting of a heroically mounted Benito Mussolini. When we stepped outside, Carmine positioned himself under a trumpet-shaped loudspeaker and posed for a photograph. He was writing a book about the Canadian poetic canon and wanted the world to hear him. Instead, I photographed him under leaves standing in for the traditional poet's laurel and a chalk outline of the sun subbing for the amplified voice of the muse.

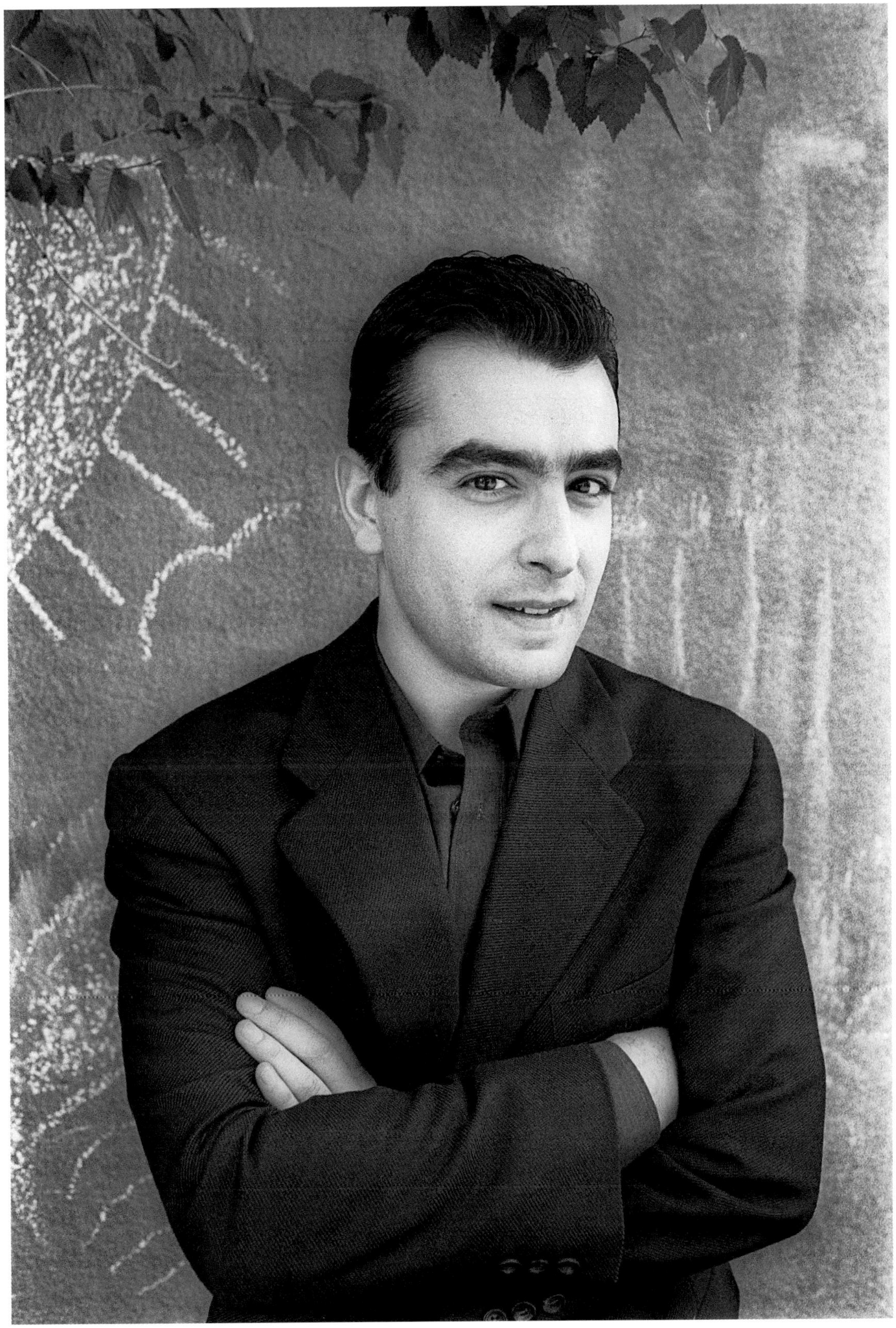

Mikhail Iossel in his first home in Canada
on Rue Fabre, Plateau Mont-Royal, May 2005

MIKHAIL'S BASEMENT OFFICE in his family's apartment was entirely white and held a computer workstation, a few shelves of books and curios, and a single bed with a metal frame. Although it struck me as penitential, the room was quiet and not uncomfortable. My flash bounced evenly off the white walls, providing lighting that looked as artificial as that of a studio set. While we talked, his computer played a Moscow radio station from the internet. The curios on his shelves included ironic political memorabilia from the USSR and an intensely soulful author portrait of Mikhail as a young man. The portrait was made during the time when he was a *samizdat* publisher and was under scrutiny by the KGB. When Mikhail eventually saw the photograph I made, his brow creased as he studied it. "I want to ask," he said. "Is this the way you see me?"

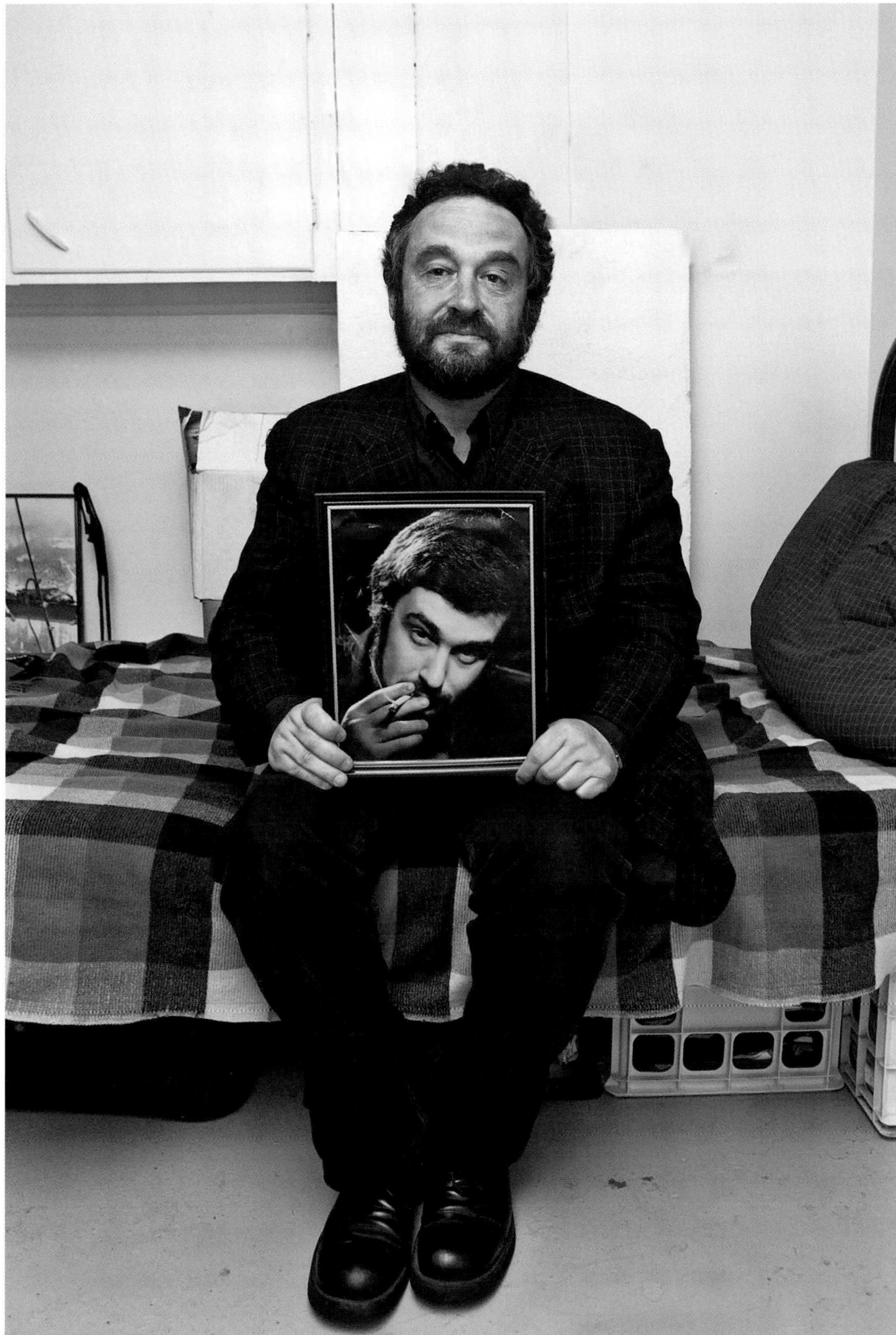

Mary di Michele in her living room
on Beaconsfield Avenue in Notre-Dame-de-Grâce, June 2000

Mary had recently purchased her first house and was preoccupied with the expense of putting on a new roof and the demanding care of elderly parents. She smiled only briefly and nervously while I photographed her, always looking quite directly, yet entirely without challenge, into the lens. She was even content to have her photographs taken in the garage, where she was dwarfed by her parents' stored furniture. I thought that she would scramble to remove the fallen poster in her living room that declared "Down By Law," which might be seen to offer an inadvertent comment on her current domestic situation, but she appeared not to notice. "It may not be the most flattering picture of me," she later said, "but it's the best photograph."

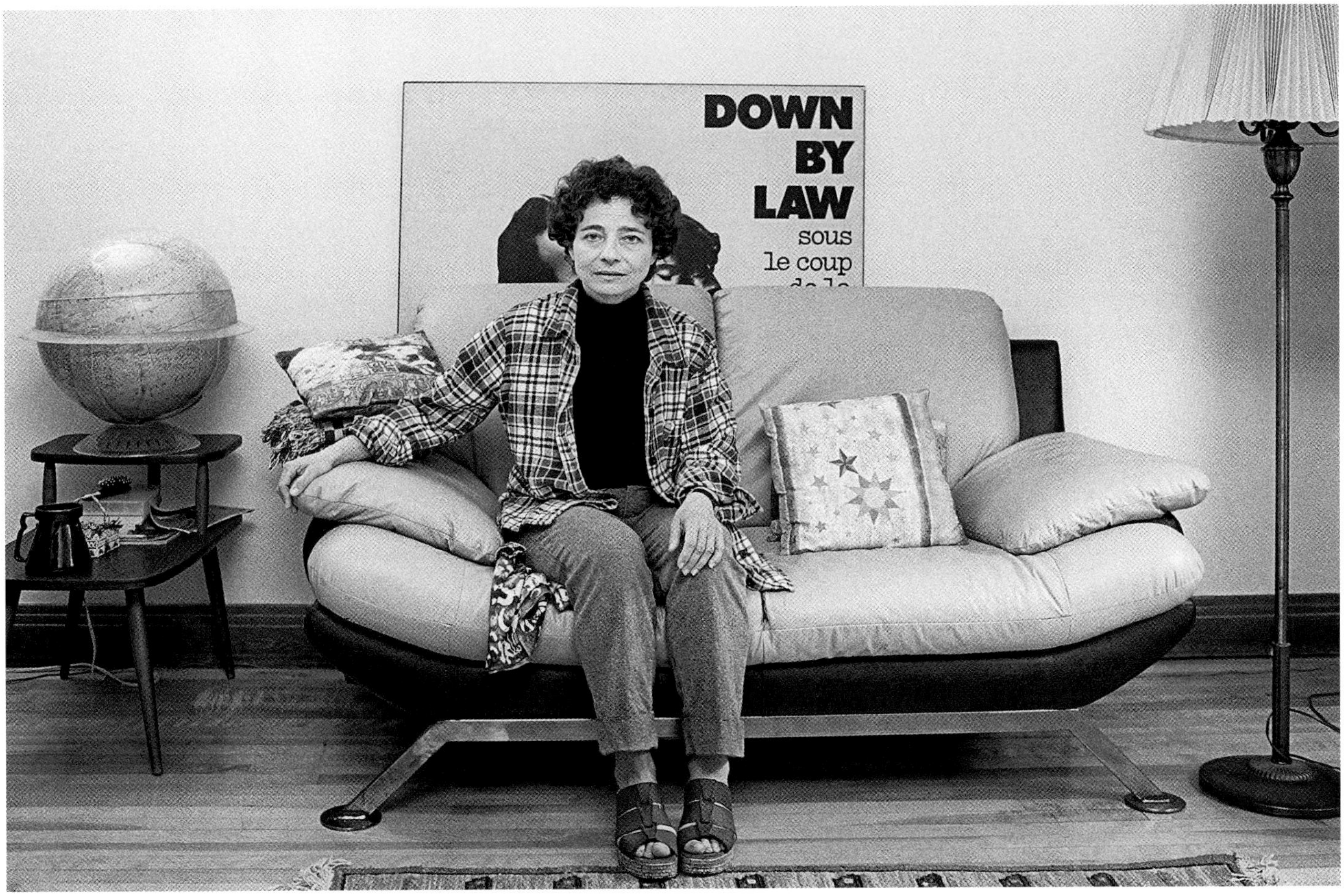
DOWN
BY
LAW
sous
le coup

Katia Gruibisic in her partner's music room,
avenue de l'Esplanade, Plateau Mont-Royal, April 2008

Katia stood in the centre of the room and reached toward the top of a double bass that was almost a foot taller than she was. Another lay beached in its huge case in the long hallway that organizes many Montreal apartments. "We have three of those whales," she said. We talked about vocation and avocation and her current translation work, but she only smiled when I asked her how many languages she now spoke. "A few," is all she would say. Instead, she told me a lengthy joke, in a recently acquired language, Spanish, about a woman with a flag on her derriere. Katia laughed when she discovered that she had forgotten the Spanish word for "flag." The topic of language led to her musing on the fact that her rural Croatian relatives weren't bothered when she had a drink with the boys because she was accepted as an "American" woman. Yet, a male Croatian writer had recently treated her like "a porcelain idiot." A few days after our shoot, she wrote me, "I hate the attributions of woman writer, women *whatevers*, feeling like we ought to be past that ... 'Flag', by the way, is *bandera*."

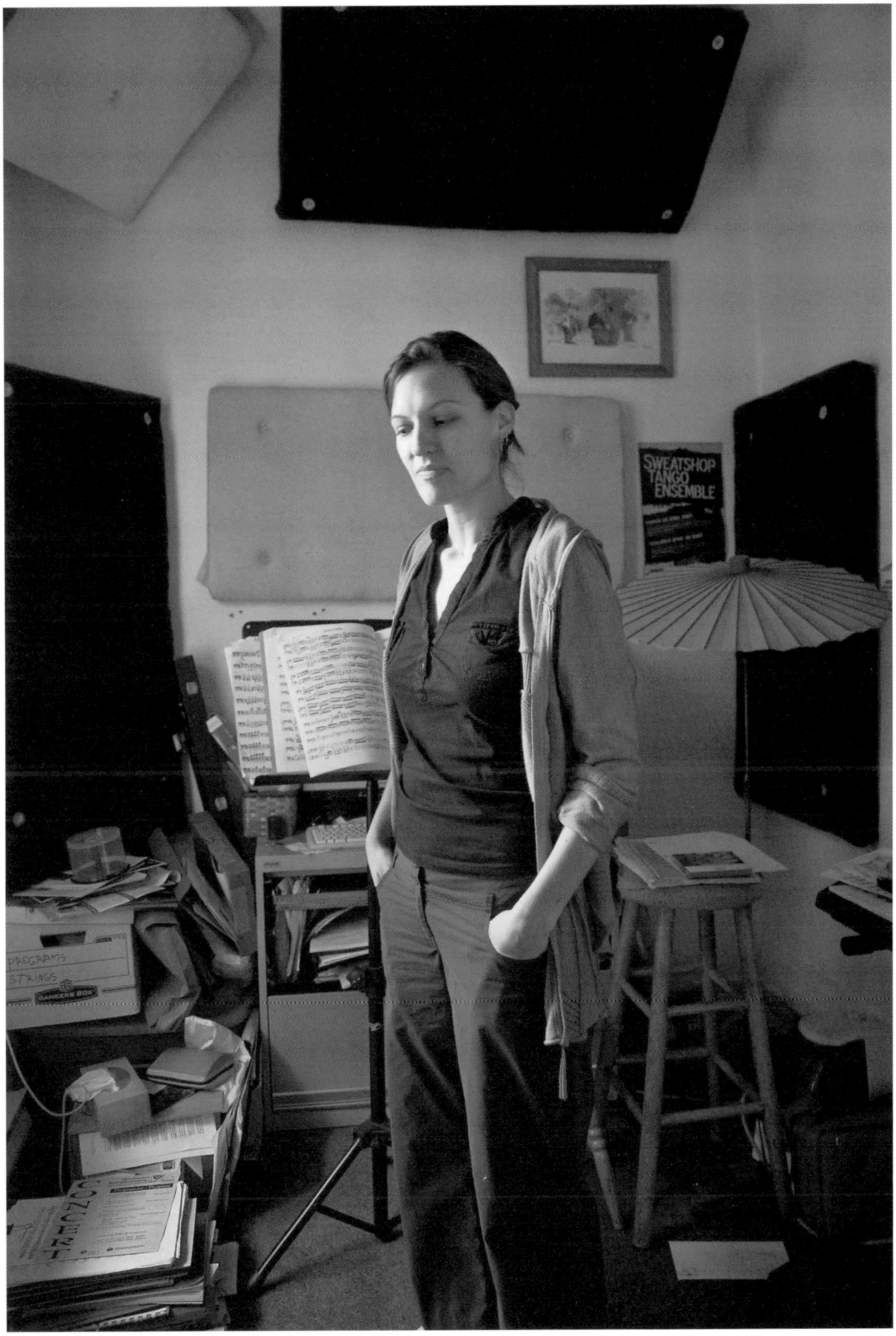
SWEATSHOP
TANGO
ENSEMBLE

DAVID McGIMPSEY IN HIS RUE VILLENEUVE APARTMENT, PLATEAU MONT-ROYAL, APRIL 2003

DAVID AND I HAD BEEN DISCUSSING the possibility of a portrait for a year or so, and he had always said that he would like to be photographed in a Future Shop in front of a wall of television screens. He wanted to be seen in the context of the aggressive, endlessly multiplying, and confusing world of public entertainment. Even though he had grown up the son of an east-end Montreal oil refinery worker, the imaginative world he occupied was devotedly American. His television room displayed two paintings, both of Elvis on black velvet, while the television itself was guarded by a Colonel Sanders statue and a Marlboro ash tray on a pedestal. David's workroom, where he also kept his guitar, was a shrine to American pop: Charlie's Angels, Jughead, and Ronald McDonald, among others, joined Elvis. Despite this self-conscious construction of a cultural environment, there was nothing got-up, and nothing very self-protective, about David himself. When we finished shooting, he said, with a gentle ripple of laughter, "When you process these, can you do just one thing? Make me slim."

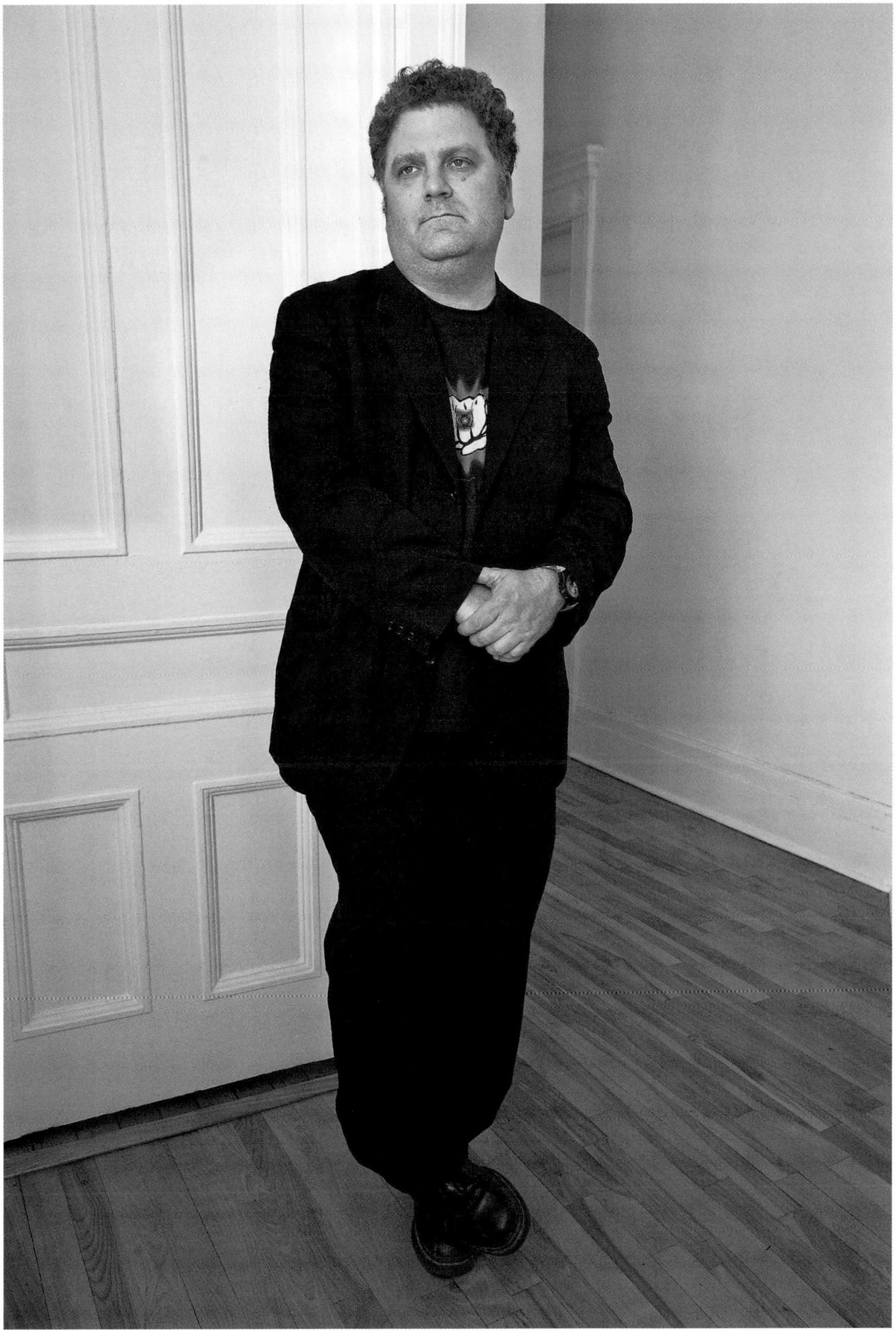

EDWARD O. PHILLIPS IN HIS DOWNTOWN APARTMENT ON SHERBROOKE STREET, MONTREAL, MAY 2003

MY FIRST VIEW OF THE GRACIOUS and gentlemanly Phillips was at a party where he unexpectedly turned on his heel and left after having been introduced to a reviewer who had trounced one of his genteel mysteries. The Phillips I met next greeted me at the door to his apartment and lauded the security system in his mid-rise building, a few blocks from the Montreal Museum of Fine Art. His apartment was done in creams and whites that contrasted with the reflective black wall behind a grand piano. The hallways were hung with subtle and expressive drawings of a young woman who had modelled for him. Phillips' partner, whom I never met, worked in a room accessible by a glass-walled balcony that segregated it from the rest of the apartment. Overall, my impression of the lives that took place in Phillips' apartment was one of industriousness and highly organized leisure.

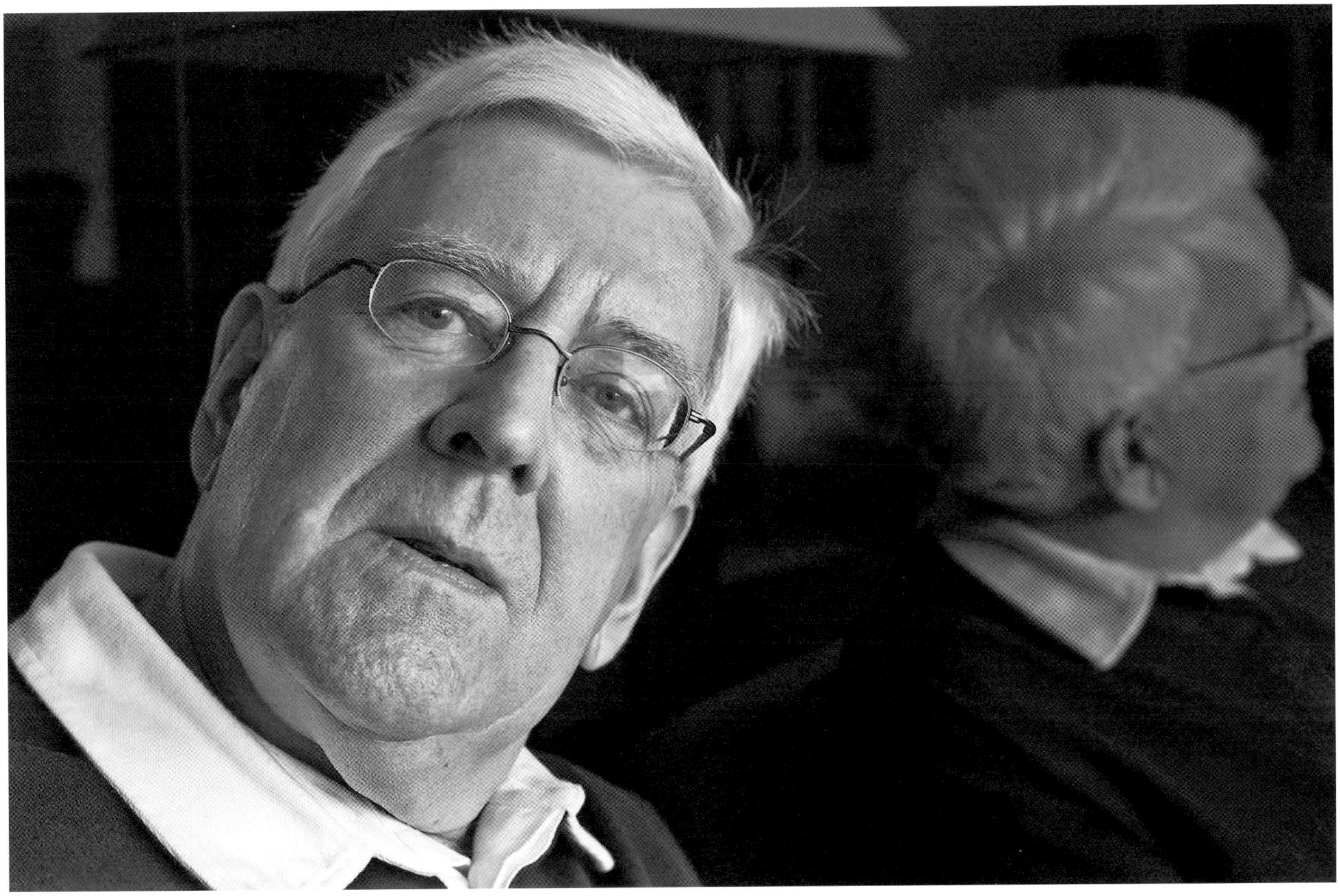

TREVOR FERGUSON AT HIS HOUSE

IN THE TOWN OF HUDSON, APRIL 2001

THE DAY THIS PHOTOGRAPH WAS MADE, I met Trevor and another writer, a friend we had in common, for lunch. Trevor, who always seemed to be in an expansive and confident mood, was enjoying the success of a *policier* called *Ice Lake* that he had just published under a pseudonym, John Farrow. Our common friend was a less successful writer whom I had just photographed and who found it so excruciatingly difficult to face the camera that we had to conclude the shoot prematurely. After lunch, Trevor posed in an unfinished bedroom, a basement workshop, and a chilly side porch. We found our best location in a room with a bewildering array of colours and patterns. Later, when our writer friend saw those images, he said, in tones of warning, that Trevor was brilliant at controlling the ways he let the world see him. I'm not sure what's wrong with that. Trevor wrote more novels and moved into theatre and film.

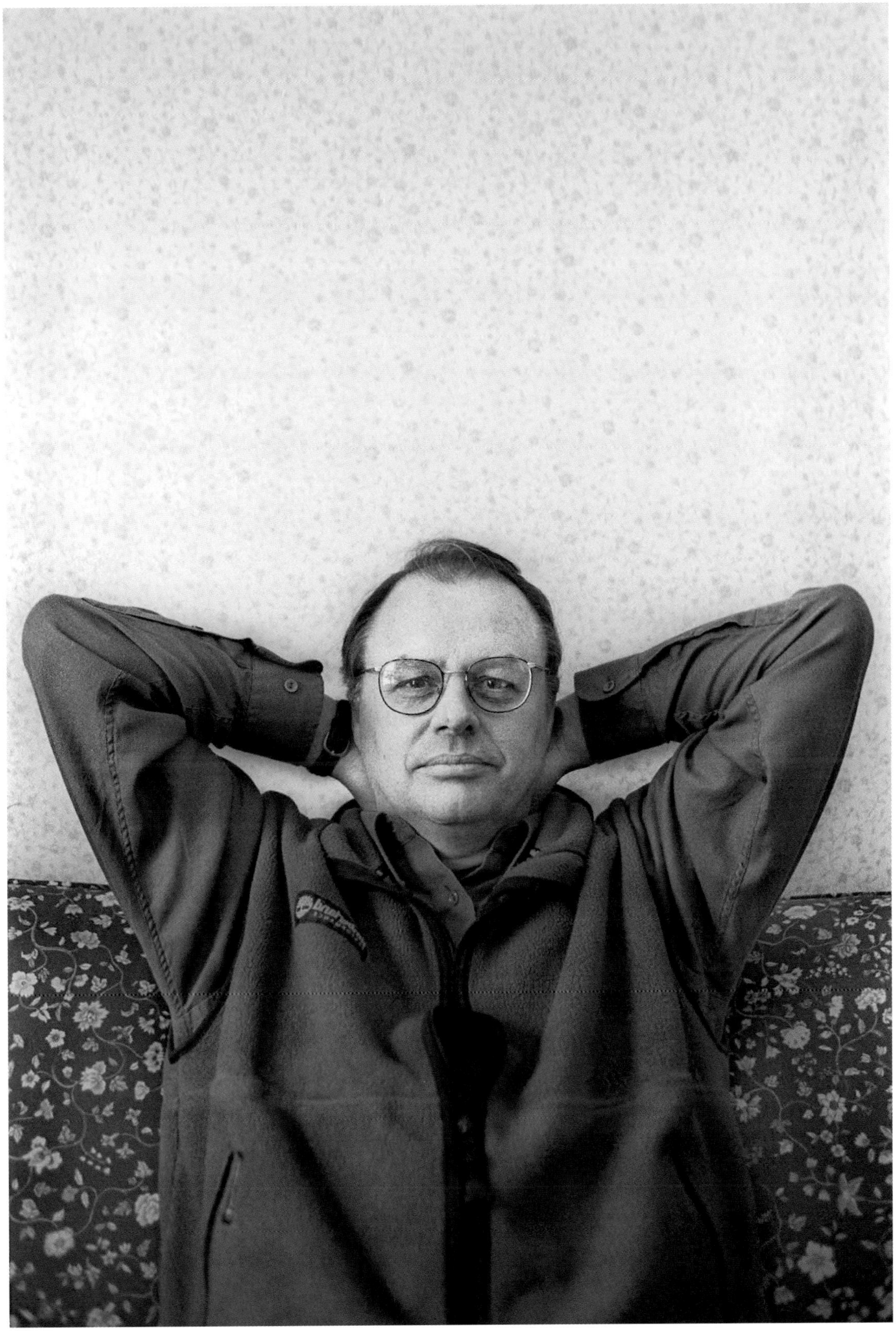

Tess Fragoulis at La Paryse

on rue Ontario Est in Plateau Mont-Royal, September 2001

I was once at a party that had started to break up around one in the morning when Tess walked in the door wearing a perfectly tailored fifties dress with a mickey of good scotch miraculously clinging to her arm under a puffy sleeve. People stopped leaving—at least long enough to get a look at the new arrival. When I photograph her, the images we produce typically have a studied and ironic quality of chic. Tess in an outfit with a white fur collar, sitting under a Coca Cola sign in front of a pistol. Tess in a sleekly shape-hugging pantsuit outside a mechanic's shop. Once, however, when I photographed her at her apartment, she introduced me to her beloved dog, Dante, and prepared us a delicious lunch. Out of role on that day, she sat under a collection of dried herbs hanging from a plaster arch over the kitchen while we discussed the music of poor Greek residents of Turkey in the nineteen-twenties. When we toured the apartment, she even let me photograph her pretending to do her ironing, although she said, in tones of dismay that sounded genuine, "I don't know why I'm letting you do this!"

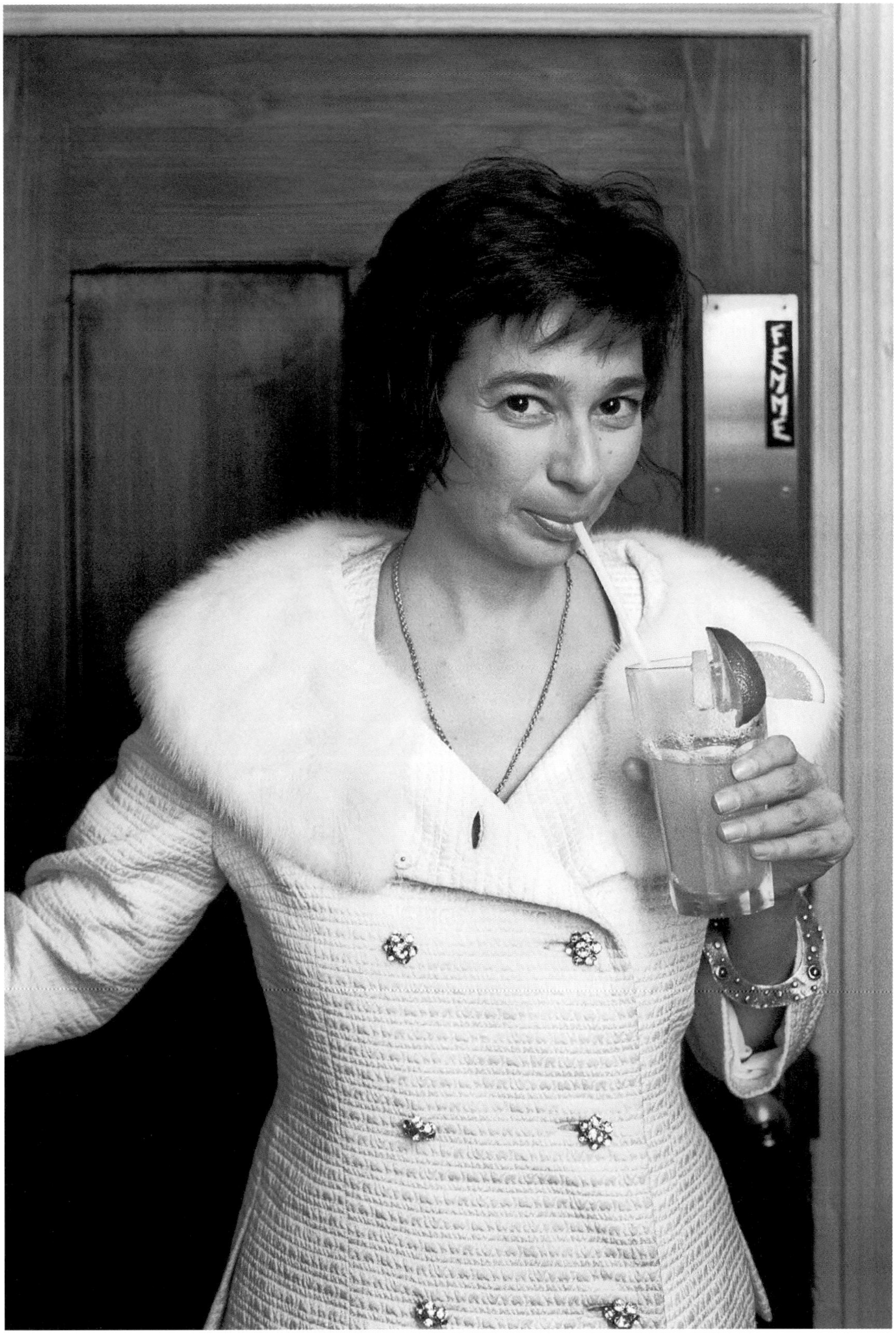
FEMME

JOEL YANOFSKY AT HIS HOME
ON GRAND AVENUE IN NOTRE-DAME-DE-GRÂCE, AUGUST 2003

I MET JOEL AT THE CORNER of Fairmount and Clark on Plateau Mont-Royal, close to the Hassidim of nearby Outremont and the famous Fairmount Bagel bakery. He had just published a book on Mordecai Richler called *Mordecai and Me*, and since we were on Richler's old territory we looked for interesting settings in the neighbourhood. Every location we considered only evoked the voluminous and dull catalogue of images that have come to stand for this storied period of Montreal history. In an alley, we discovered a white, spray-painted outline of a human form and Joel obligingly stood inside it, willing to inhabit for a moment the ghost of Mordecai Richler. As a journalist, he understood the appetite for simple and declarative images, but as an artist, he was wary of them. Finally, he drove us to his home. There, he bounced on a trampoline, got into bed and wrapped himself in a quilt, stared into a mirror, played with his child's toys, and hugged his wife.

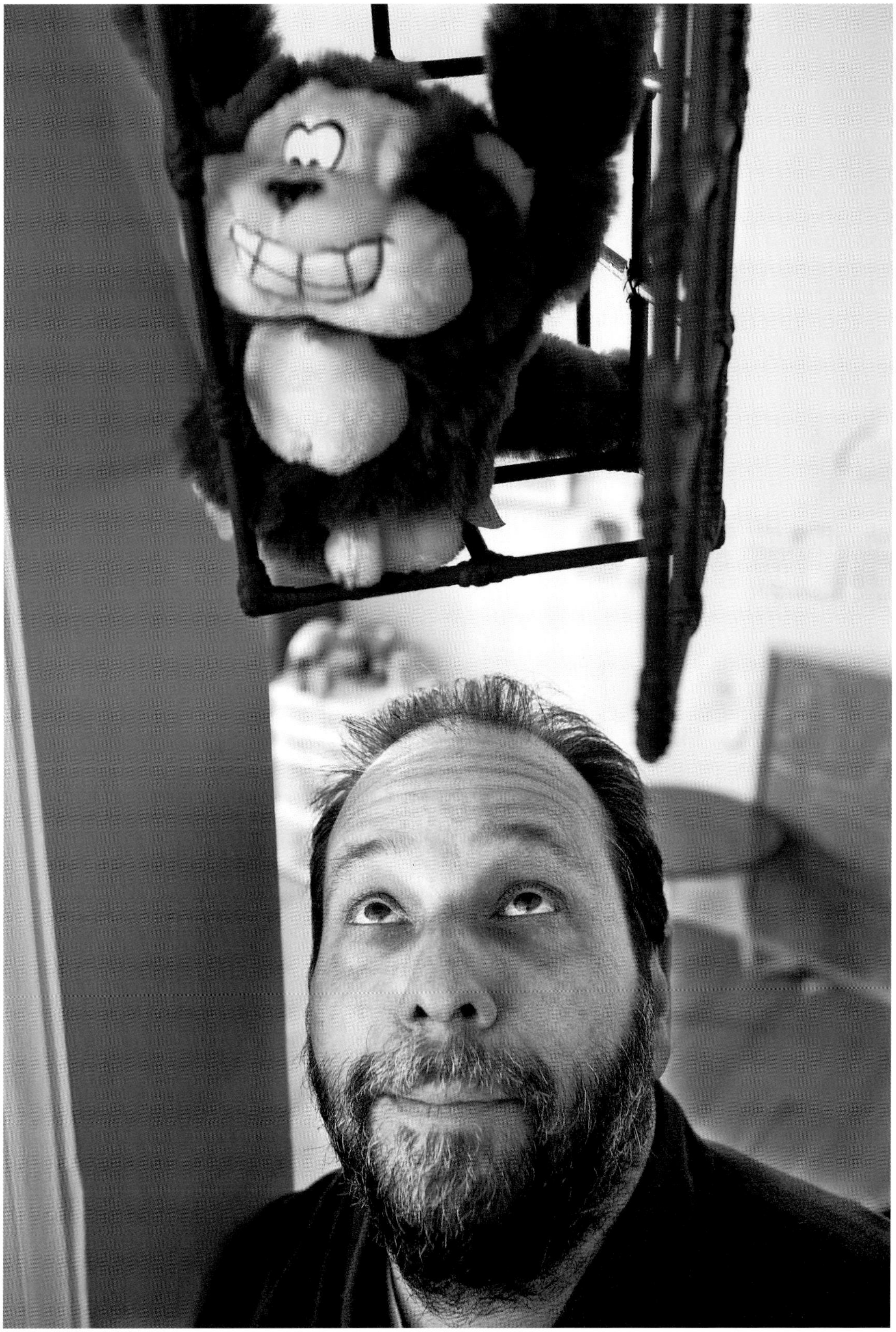

PORTRAITURE AT HOME

TECHNICAL NOTES

ALL THE PORTRAITS IN THIS BOOK were made with what used to be called "hand cameras," to distinguish them from large format, tripod-mounted cameras. In the earliest days of photography, the subject was positioned with the help of an iron frame guiding the spine and supporting the back of the head, and exposures could last several minutes, even in direct sunlight. Many early subjects wrote about their eyes streaming with tears because the camera operator encouraged them to remain still and not blink. Some of the images in this book were made in much less than a hundred thousandth of the time it would have taken in 1840. Time is the central factor in determining the changes in the look of photographic portraits over the history of the form.

In photographing for this book, I told all the writers that the photographs would be made where they lived, worked, or played and, for many, home met all three requirements. I also told them that we would try to avoid bookcases, bricks, and computer screens, three things that everyone seemed to have in abundance. After speaking with the subject for a few minutes, I would place my camera in his or her hands and ask for a picture of myself. Most people, conditioned by the modern digital camera, looked for a screen instead of a finder and had to be coaxed to look into the eyepiece. When the picture was taken and glanced at (it was briefly visible on a screen), the camera would be handed back to me with what often seemed like a sense of considerable relief.

I would then spend an hour or more finding locations in the writer's house or favourite haunt, searching for the light or the elements of design to bring a frame to life, and discussing literature, writing, and whatever might come up. (That, by the way, partly explains the absence of French-speaking writers in the book. Conversation had to be quick, and varied cultural references at hand. I couldn't have brought this off in French.)

When I began the project, I used a 35 mm camera and Tri-X film, sometimes shooting it at ISO 400 and pushing it in development to cope with the frequently low light. By the time the project concluded, I was using a 35 mm digital camera, shooting colour RAW files, processing them digitally, and producing monochrome prints on archival baryta paper with an inkjet printer using pure pigment inks. The somewhat ostentatious art world name for this kind of print is *giclée*, from the unostentatious French word *gicleur* or "nozzle." The several leaps in technology that occurred during the life of the project are reflected in different tonal distributions and degrees of smoothness in individual photographs in this book.

I tried to keep the lighting natural, or at least natural-looking. Window light models the features exceptionally well, and the diminishing intensity of light as it moves through a room creates a sense of depth. When there was no useable light, I would bounce a flash off a ceiling or wall. In that instance, the flat, even light resulted in a bland image, and I spent many hours performing the digital equivalent of dodging and burning to bring out richness of tone and shape.

The future of portraiture will also be determined, in part, by time. Movie and still technologies are converging and it will be possible to follow a subject continuously with a movie camera that produces images of such high quality that each one might also be considered a printable "still." Portraiture that uses a device capable of capturing 30 or images every second will supplant photography that depends on a quick eye and hand.

Photographic portraits, literary or otherwise, are not just there for the taking. It was, I think, that implicit understanding of the photographer's role that made my subjects relinquish the camera I had given them with a feeling of relief. When they looked into the viewfinder, they couldn't see a portrait, just the ordinary disarray of the world.

alphabetical list of portraits